CALEB ROSS

Asynchronous Programming With C 12 And .NET 8

Copyright © 2024 by Caleb Ross

All rights reserved. No part of this publication may be reproduced, stored or transmitted in any form or by any means, electronic, mechanical, photocopying, recording, scanning, or otherwise without written permission from the publisher. It is illegal to copy this book, post it to a website, or distribute it by any other means without permission.

First edition

This book was professionally typeset on Reedsy.
Find out more at reedsy.com

Contents

Introduction	1
Chapter 1: Getting Started with Asynchronous Programming in...	8
Chapter 2: Deep Dive into Asynchronous Programming with C#12	16
Chapter 3: Performance Optimization in Asynchronous...	27
Chapter 4: Best Practices for Managing Asynchronous Code in...	39
Chapter 4: Performance Optimization in Asynchronous...	49
Chapter 5: Advanced Techniques in Asynchronous Programming...	61
Chapter 6: Testing Asynchronous Code in C#12	73
Chapter 7: Best Practices for Designing Asynchronous APIs in...	84
Chapter 8: Real-World Scenarios and Case Studies in...	93
Chapter 9: Best Practices for Optimizing Asynchronous...	105
Chapter 10: Advanced Topics in Asynchronous Programming with...	117
Chapter 11: Future Directions in Asynchronous Programming...	128
Chapter 12: Conclusion and Key Takeaways from Asynchronous...	135
Chapter 13: Implementing Real-World Applications of...	141
Chapter 14: Best Practices for Maintaining Asynchronous Code...	155
Chapter 15: Emerging Trends and Future Directions in...	165
Conclusion	173

Introduction

Overview of Asynchronous Programming in Modern Applications As software systems grow in complexity and scale, developers face increasing pressure to build applications that are responsive, efficient, and capable of handling multiple tasks concurrently. Traditional synchronous programming, where each task waits for the previous one to complete before proceeding, often leads to bottlenecks, slow response times, and unoptimized resource usage. This challenge becomes especially pronounced in modern, distributed systems where cloud services, network requests, and user interactions occur in parallel.

This is where asynchronous programming plays a pivotal role. Asynchronous programming allows a program to perform multiple tasks simultaneously without blocking the main thread. By decoupling the execution of a task from the flow of control, asynchronous methods enable applications to remain responsive, even when handling time-consuming operations such as file I/O, database queries, or API requests.

In modern applications, especially those that demand high performance and scalability, asynchronous programming has become indispensable. Whether you are building a web application that handles thousands of concurrent requests, a real-time communication tool, or a data-intensive service that processes streams of information, asynchronous programming allows your system to operate efficiently without unnecessary delays.

The growing prevalence of cloud-native applications, microservices, and real-time systems has only accelerated the need for robust and efficient asynchronous programming paradigms. From web servers to mobile apps and desktop software, asynchronous techniques provide the foundation for responsiveness, scalability, and efficient resource management.

Why Asynchronous Programming Matters in C#12 and .NET 8

With each iteration, the C# language and .NET framework have introduced significant enhancements to support asynchronous programming. The introduction of the async and await keywords in C# marked a turning point for developers, providing a clean and intuitive way to write asynchronous code without the complexity of callbacks and state machines. Over the years, these constructs have evolved, making asynchronous programming more efficient and easier to implement.

In C#12 and .NET 8, Microsoft continues to push the boundaries of what asynchronous programming can achieve. These versions introduce powerful new features that address common pain points faced by developers and streamline the development process. Let's explore some of the key advancements:

1. **Task-based Asynchronous Pattern (TAP) Improvements**: While the Task-based Asynchronous Pattern has been a cornerstone of asynchronous programming in C#, C#12 brings further refinements. Enhancements in task scheduling and the ability to handle high-throughput, low-latency tasks make it easier to build scalable systems.

2. **Asynchronous Streams**: C#12 continues to build on asynchronous streams (IAsyncEnumerable<T>), which allow developers to iterate over asynchronous data sources efficiently. This is particularly useful in real-time applications, where data is continuously streamed from a server or another external source. Instead of blocking while waiting for data, you can process it asynchronously, as it arrives, without holding up the main thread.

3. **Improved Exception Handling**: One of the key challenges in asynchronous programming is dealing with exceptions and error handling. C#12 improves exception propagation, making it easier to catch and

manage exceptions in asynchronous code. This results in more predictable and manageable error handling, even in complex, asynchronous workflows.
4. **Enhanced Performance**: .NET 8 introduces significant performance improvements, particularly for asynchronous programming. From reducing overhead in asynchronous method calls to more efficient memory usage and threading models, .NET 8 ensures that asynchronous operations run faster and with lower resource consumption. This is crucial in high-performance applications, such as microservices, cloud-based APIs, and real-time systems.
5. **Task-Cancellation Improvements**: In long-running tasks, cancellation tokens are essential to prevent wasteful operations when a user or system cancels a task. C#12 and .NET 8 improve the management of task cancellations, making it easier to write responsive and resource-efficient applications.
6. **Integration with Modern Architectures**: As microservices and cloud-native applications continue to dominate software development, the need for robust asynchronous programming patterns has grown. C#12 and .NET 8 provide better integration with cloud services, making it easier to build distributed systems where tasks are offloaded to external services or distributed across multiple nodes.

For developers, mastering asynchronous programming in C#12 and .NET 8 is no longer optional. It's essential for building modern, scalable, and high-performance applications. By understanding the latest asynchronous patterns and leveraging the new features in these versions, developers can write code that is not only more efficient but also more maintainable and robust.

Who This Book is For

This book is designed for a wide range of readers, including:

1. **Professional Developers**: Whether you're a seasoned C# developer or transitioning from another language, this book provides the depth

and clarity needed to master asynchronous programming in C#12 and .NET 8. You'll learn how to optimize your code for performance, avoid common pitfalls, and implement best practices that are critical for building modern, scalable applications.

2. **Software Architects**: If you design large-scale systems or cloud-based architectures, this book will help you integrate asynchronous programming patterns into your solutions. It covers everything from designing responsive APIs to building microservices that efficiently handle concurrent operations.

3. **Intermediate Programmers**: If you're familiar with C# but new to asynchronous programming, this book will guide you through the essential concepts. It starts with the basics and gradually introduces more complex topics, ensuring that you have a solid foundation before tackling advanced asynchronous programming techniques.

4. **Backend Developers**: Asynchronous programming is especially important in backend development, where server-side applications need to handle high traffic volumes and concurrent requests. This book provides detailed examples and best practices for building high-performance, asynchronous APIs and services.

5. **Cloud-Native Developers**: For those working in cloud environments (e.g., Azure, AWS, Google Cloud), understanding asynchronous programming is crucial for building scalable, fault-tolerant systems. This book explores how asynchronous programming fits into modern cloud-native architectures and microservices design.

6. **Real-Time Systems Engineers**: If you're developing systems that require real-time responsiveness (e.g., gaming, live-streaming, or IoT applications), this book provides the tools you need to write non-blocking, asynchronous code that ensures your systems remain performant even under heavy loads.

7. **Students and Learners**: For students and learners aspiring to become proficient in C# development, this book introduces key asynchronous programming concepts in an accessible and practical way. It's structured to help you apply theoretical knowledge through real-world projects.

INTRODUCTION

How to Use This Book

This book is structured to provide a comprehensive understanding of asynchronous programming in C#12 and .NET 8, starting with fundamental concepts and progressing to more advanced techniques. Each chapter builds upon the previous one, creating a natural learning progression. Here's how you can best use this book:

1. **Start with the Basics**: If you're new to asynchronous programming, begin with the early chapters that introduce the fundamental concepts. Chapters like "Task-Based Asynchronous Programming (TAP)" and "Deep Dive into Async and Await Enhancements" are critical for building a strong foundation.
2. **Dive into Real-World Scenarios**: Throughout the book, you'll find practical examples and case studies that demonstrate how asynchronous programming is applied in modern software development. These real-world scenarios will help you see how asynchronous techniques are used in cloud computing, web development, and high-performance applications.
3. **Use the Code Examples**: The book is filled with code snippets and hands-on examples. Make sure to try them out as you read along. The best way to understand asynchronous programming is by seeing how it works in action, so experiment with the code and adapt it to your own projects.
4. **Take on the Challenges**: At the end of each chapter, you'll find exercises and coding challenges. These are designed to reinforce the concepts you've learned and push your understanding to the next level. Completing these challenges will help solidify your grasp of asynchronous programming.
5. **Refer to the Glossary**: Throughout the book, technical terms are explained as they appear, but a detailed glossary is also included at the end. If you're unfamiliar with a specific term or concept, feel free to refer to this section to get a quick explanation.
6. **Optimize for Your Needs**: Depending on your background and goals,

you may want to focus on particular sections of the book. For example, if you're primarily interested in web development, focus on chapters like "Asynchronous Programming in Web Applications." If you're working on cloud-native systems, chapters like "Async Programming in Cloud-Native Architectures" will be especially relevant.

Key Concepts and Terminology

Before diving into the more complex aspects of asynchronous programming, it's important to familiarize yourself with the following key concepts and terms. These form the foundation of asynchronous programming in C#12 and .NET 8, and you'll encounter them frequently throughout the book:

1. **Synchronous vs Asynchronous Programming**: In synchronous programming, tasks are executed sequentially, meaning that each task must wait for the previous one to complete before it can start. In asynchronous programming, tasks can be executed concurrently, without waiting for the previous task to finish, allowing for more efficient use of resources.
2. **Task-based Asynchronous Pattern (TAP)**: TAP is the standard pattern for asynchronous programming in C#. It uses Task and Task<T> types to represent asynchronous operations. The async and await keywords are used to write asynchronous code in a way that is easy to understand and maintain.
3. **Task**: A Task represents an operation that will complete in the future. It can be awaited, canceled, or combined with other tasks. Tasks are the building blocks of asynchronous programming in C#.
4. **Task.Run()**: This method allows you to offload a piece of work to run asynchronously on a separate thread, freeing up the main thread to continue processing other tasks.
5. **Await**: The await keyword is used to asynchronously wait for the completion of a task. It suspends the execution of the method until the awaited task is finished, allowing other tasks to execute in the meantime.

6. **IAsyncEnumerable**: Introduced in C#8 and enhanced in C#12, IAsyncEnumerable represents a collection of items that can be asynchronously enumerated. It is useful for scenarios where data is streamed asynchronously, such as reading from a network or a database.
7. **ValueTask**: A ValueTask is a more efficient alternative to Task when working with asynchronous methods that are frequently completed synchronously. It minimizes memory allocations, making it a useful tool for optimizing performance in high-throughput applications.
8. **Thread Pool**: The thread pool is a collection of reusable threads that can be used to execute asynchronous tasks. Efficient management of the thread pool is key to ensuring the scalability and responsiveness of asynchronous applications.
9. **Cancellation Token**: A CancellationToken allows you to signal that an asynchronous operation should be canceled. It is used to gracefully stop long-running tasks without leaving the system in an inconsistent state.
10. **Deadlock**: In asynchronous programming, deadlocks occur when two or more tasks are waiting for each other to complete, resulting in an infinite wait state. Understanding how to avoid deadlocks is critical for writing robust asynchronous code.

Chapter 1: Getting Started with Asynchronous Programming in C#12

1.1 Understanding Synchronous vs. Asynchronous Programming

Before diving into asynchronous programming, it's essential to understand how it contrasts with synchronous programming. These two paradigms handle task execution in fundamentally different ways, impacting an application's performance, responsiveness, and resource usage.

1.1.1 What is Synchronous Programming?

In synchronous programming, tasks are executed sequentially. Each task must complete before the next one begins, meaning the program execution follows a strict, step-by-step order. This approach is straightforward and easy to reason about, but it can lead to inefficiencies, especially when dealing with I/O-bound operations.

For instance, imagine a web application that makes a call to an external API. In a synchronous system, the program would wait for the API response before continuing to the next operation. If the API takes five seconds to respond, those five seconds are spent waiting—essentially blocking the entire application from performing other tasks.

This approach is problematic when building applications that must handle multiple concurrent requests, perform real-time updates, or interact with users interactively. The program becomes less responsive, leading to poor user experiences and inefficient resource utilization.

1.1.2 What is Asynchronous Programming?

In contrast, asynchronous programming allows multiple tasks to run concurrently without blocking the program's flow. Instead of waiting for a task to finish, the program can continue executing other tasks while the first task completes in the background. When the asynchronous operation finishes, the program can handle the result or error without interrupting its workflow.

This approach is highly beneficial in scenarios where operations involve external systems (such as database queries, web requests, or file I/O) that could take an indeterminate amount of time. Asynchronous programming allows an application to remain responsive even when performing time-consuming tasks.

Example: Imagine a web server that needs to process multiple user requests simultaneously. In a synchronous model, the server would process each request one by one, meaning that users would have to wait their turn. In an asynchronous model, the server can begin processing a request and move on to others while waiting for operations (such as database access) to complete. This leads to faster, more responsive systems.

The key advantage of asynchronous programming is that it allows you to build non-blocking, highly responsive applications that can scale efficiently. In modern distributed systems, which rely heavily on APIs, microservices, and cloud platforms, asynchronous programming is a necessity.

1.2 Basic Concepts: Tasks, Threads, and Event Loops

To understand asynchronous programming in C#, it's crucial to grasp some core concepts that form the foundation of how tasks are managed, executed, and coordinated. These include **tasks**, **threads**, and **event loops**. Let's break each of these down.

1.2.1 Tasks

In C#, a **task** represents an asynchronous operation. The Task class is part of the **Task-based Asynchronous Pattern (TAP)**, and it allows developers to work with asynchronous code in a structured and predictable manner.

A task can either be completed immediately, run asynchronously in the background, or await the result of another task. The ability to chain tasks together (using the async and await keywords) allows developers to create complex asynchronous workflows without manually managing threads.

Tasks are extremely versatile:
- They can represent operations that return a result (Task<T>).
- They can be awaited, which means the program waits for them to finish without blocking the main thread.
- They can be canceled using **cancellation tokens**, ensuring that the application doesn't waste resources on tasks that are no longer needed.

Example:

```csharp
Copy code
public async Task<string> GetDataAsync(string url)
{
    using var client = new HttpClient();
    return await client.GetStringAsync(url);
}
```

Here, the GetDataAsync method runs asynchronously and returns a Task<string>, which represents the result of the HTTP request. The await keyword ensures that the method waits for the task to complete, but it doesn't block the calling thread.

1.2.2 Threads

A **thread** is the basic unit of execution in a program. When a task is started, it runs on a thread, which can either be part of the **thread pool** or manually created. Each thread operates independently, meaning multiple threads can execute code simultaneously.

In asynchronous programming, threads are a key resource. However, rather than manually creating and managing threads, the .NET runtime efficiently handles threads through the thread pool, allowing tasks to run asynchronously without explicitly dealing with the complexities of multithreading.

CHAPTER 1: GETTING STARTED WITH ASYNCHRONOUS PROGRAMMING IN...

1.2.3 Event Loops

The **event loop** is a design pattern used to handle asynchronous tasks in a non-blocking way. It continually checks for new tasks to execute, monitors for completed tasks, and schedules callbacks for tasks that have finished execution.

In C# asynchronous programming, the event loop plays a role behind the scenes, coordinating the execution of tasks. It allows the main thread to remain responsive while waiting for background tasks to complete. By leveraging the event loop, asynchronous operations are scheduled and handled efficiently without blocking the entire application.

Understanding the interplay between tasks, threads, and the event loop is essential for writing efficient asynchronous code. Tasks run on threads, and the event loop manages the execution of asynchronous operations, ensuring that your application remains responsive and scalable.

1.3 Asynchronous Patterns in C#: Evolution from APM, EAP, to TAP

Asynchronous programming in C# has evolved significantly over time. Earlier patterns, while functional, introduced complexity and were often difficult to implement correctly. Let's briefly review the evolution of asynchronous patterns in C#.

1.3.1 Asynchronous Programming Model (APM)

The **Asynchronous Programming Model (APM)**, also known as the **Begin/End pattern**, was one of the earliest methods for asynchronous programming in .NET. This pattern involved manually defining methods that followed a specific structure, such as BeginOperation and EndOperation, which allowed the developer to initiate and conclude asynchronous operations.

Example:

```csharp
Copy code
var asyncResult = fileStream.BeginRead(buffer, 0, buffer.Length, null, null);
int bytesRead = fileStream.EndRead(asyncResult);
```

While APM allowed for asynchronous execution, it was cumbersome, error-prone, and hard to maintain, especially in more complex scenarios.

1.3.2 Event-based Asynchronous Pattern (EAP)

The **Event-based Asynchronous Pattern (EAP)** built on APM and aimed to simplify asynchronous programming by providing an event-driven model. It introduced the concept of events being raised when an asynchronous operation completed, simplifying how developers managed long-running tasks.

Example:

```csharp
Copy code
client.DownloadFileCompleted += new
AsyncCompletedEventHandler(DownloadFileCallback);
client.DownloadFileAsync(new Uri("http://example.com/file.txt"));
```

While EAP was easier to use than APM, it still suffered from complexity in scenarios involving multiple asynchronous operations or chaining tasks together. Additionally, it could lead to "callback hell"—a situation where deeply nested callbacks make code difficult to read and maintain.

1.3.3 Task-based Asynchronous Pattern (TAP)

The **Task-based Asynchronous Pattern (TAP)**, introduced with .NET 4.0, revolutionized asynchronous programming in C#. TAP uses the Task and Task<T> classes to represent asynchronous operations. These tasks can be awaited using the async and await keywords, allowing for cleaner, more readable code without complex callback structures.

TAP also integrates seamlessly with modern C# features like LINQ and provides native support for asynchronous programming without the need for manually creating threads or handling callbacks.

Example:

```csharp
Copy code
```

CHAPTER 1: GETTING STARTED WITH ASYNCHRONOUS PROGRAMMING IN...

```
public async Task<string> FetchDataAsync(string url)
{
    using var client = new HttpClient();
    return await client.GetStringAsync(url);
}
```

With TAP, developers can now write asynchronous code that looks very similar to synchronous code. This makes it easier to understand and maintain, reducing the likelihood of bugs and improving overall productivity.

1.4 Overview of the Async and Await Keywords

Introduced in C# 5.0 and refined in later versions, the async and await keywords are at the heart of asynchronous programming in C#. They enable developers to write asynchronous code that is both readable and maintainable. Understanding how these keywords work is essential for working with modern asynchronous patterns in C#.

1.4.1 The Async Keyword

The async keyword is used to mark a method as asynchronous. When a method is declared with async, it signals that it may contain one or more await expressions. However, an async method does not necessarily have to contain await—but if it doesn't, it will run synchronously.

An important thing to note is that async methods should return a Task, Task<T>, or void (in rare cases, such as event handlers). Returning a Task allows the method to be awaited by other asynchronous code, making it part of a larger asynchronous workflow.

1.4.2 The Await Keyword

The await keyword is used within an async method to pause execution until the awaited task completes. However, unlike traditional synchronous waiting, await doesn't block the calling thread. Instead, it allows other tasks to continue executing while the awaited task completes in the background.

This non-blocking behavior is what makes await so powerful. It ensures that your application remains responsive, even when performing long-running operations such as network requests or database queries.

Example:

```csharp
Copy code
public async Task<int> DownloadDataAsync(string url)
{
    using var client = new HttpClient();
    var data = await client.GetStringAsync(url);
    return data.Length;
}
```

In the example above, the method fetches data asynchronously from a URL. The await keyword ensures that the method waits for the data to be downloaded before returning the length of the data, but the thread is not blocked while waiting.

1.5 Setup: Tools and IDEs for C#12 and .NET 8 Development

Now that we've introduced the concepts of asynchronous programming, it's time to set up your development environment. To effectively write and test asynchronous code in C#12 and .NET 8, you'll need the right tools and IDEs.

1.5.1 Installing .NET 8 SDK

To get started with C#12 and .NET 8, you'll need to install the .NET 8 SDK. You can download the latest version from the official .NET website. The SDK includes everything you need to build, run, and test applications using the .NET 8 runtime.

- Visit: https://dotnet.microsoft.com/download/dotnet/8.0
- Follow the installation instructions for your operating system (Windows, macOS, Linux).

Once installed, you can verify the installation by opening a terminal or command prompt and running the following command:

CHAPTER 1: GETTING STARTED WITH ASYNCHRONOUS PROGRAMMING IN...

```bash
Copy code
dotnet --version
```

1.5.2 Setting Up Visual Studio

Visual Studio is the recommended IDE for developing C#12 and .NET 8 applications. It provides rich support for debugging, refactoring, and performance profiling of asynchronous code.

1. Download and install the latest version of Visual Studio from the official website (https://visualstudio.microsoft.com).
2. During installation, ensure that you select the **.NET Desktop Development** and **ASP.NET and Web Development** workloads, as they include the tools and libraries needed for asynchronous programming.

1.5.3 Using Visual Studio Code

If you prefer a lightweight editor, **Visual Studio Code** (VS Code) is a popular alternative. It's free, cross-platform, and has excellent support for C# development via the **C# extension**.

1. Download VS Code from https://code.visualstudio.com.
2. Install the **C# extension** from the marketplace.
3. Configure VS Code for .NET 8 development by installing the .NET SDK and ensuring that it's recognized by the editor.

1.5.4 Debugging Asynchronous Code

Both Visual Studio and VS Code provide robust tools for debugging asynchronous code. Visual Studio's **Tasks window** allows you to track the status of running tasks and see how they interact with other parts of the application. Breakpoints, watch windows, and performance profiling are essential features for ensuring that your asynchronous code behaves as expected.

Chapter 2: Deep Dive into Asynchronous Programming with C#12

2.1 Introduction to Task-Based Asynchronous Programming (TAP) in C#12

In modern C# development, the **Task-based Asynchronous Pattern (TAP)** forms the foundation of asynchronous programming. Introduced in .NET Framework 4, TAP allows developers to work with asynchronous methods in a streamlined and structured way. Using the Task and Task<T> objects, TAP standardizes how asynchronous methods are written and consumed, and in C#12, the pattern continues to evolve, providing better control and performance.

2.1.1 Key Features of TAP in C#12

The Task-based Asynchronous Pattern offers several benefits over earlier asynchronous patterns like the Asynchronous Programming Model (APM) or the Event-based Asynchronous Pattern (EAP). Key improvements in C#12 include:

1. **Simplified Method Chaining**: The ability to chain asynchronous tasks using the async and await keywords without needing complex callback handling.
2. **Improved Exception Handling**: In TAP, exceptions are naturally propagated through tasks, making error handling simpler and more

robust in asynchronous workflows.

3. **Increased Performance in I/O-Bound Tasks**: TAP excels in handling tasks that involve I/O operations, such as network requests, file system access, and database queries. C#12 optimizes these operations even further through improved task scheduling and background processing.
4. **Support for Asynchronous Streams**: TAP in C#12 introduces refinements for asynchronous streams, allowing developers to process large or continuous data streams asynchronously without blocking the main thread.

2.1.2 Understanding Task and Task<T>

At the core of TAP are the Task and Task<T> types. A Task represents an operation that runs asynchronously, and Task<T> is a generic type that returns a value upon completion.

- **Task**: Represents an asynchronous operation that does not return a result.
- **Task<T>**: Represents an asynchronous operation that returns a result of type T.

These tasks can be awaited or chained together, allowing developers to write non-blocking code that looks similar to synchronous code.

Example:

```csharp
Copy code
public async Task ProcessDataAsync()
{
    var result = await GetDataAsync();
    await SaveDataAsync(result);
}
```

In this example, two asynchronous methods (GetDataAsync and SaveDataAsync) are awaited in sequence. The execution continues without blocking the main thread, making the code responsive and scalable.

2.2 Async Streams and IAsyncEnumerable in C#12

With the introduction of **IAsyncEnumerable** in C#8, developers gained the ability to work with asynchronous streams—data sources that produce results over time. C#12 builds on this feature, offering even more efficient ways to process streams asynchronously.

2.2.1 What is IAsyncEnumerable?

IAsyncEnumerable represents a collection of asynchronous data. It allows developers to asynchronously iterate over items using the await keyword within a foreach loop, making it ideal for scenarios like reading large datasets from databases, processing streams of data from network requests, or working with real-time data.

Example:

```csharp
Copy code
public async IAsyncEnumerable<int> GetNumbersAsync()
{
    for (int i = 1; i <= 10; i++)
    {
        await Task.Delay(1000); // Simulating asynchronous operation
        yield return i;
    }
}
```

Here, the method asynchronously returns a sequence of numbers over time. Consumers of this method can asynchronously iterate over these numbers without blocking the main thread.

2.2.2 Benefits of Asynchronous Streams

1. **Non-Blocking Iteration**: With **IAsyncEnumerable**, the data is processed as it becomes available, preventing the program from waiting for all data to be ready before continuing.
2. **Reduced Memory Consumption**: Instead of loading large data sets all

at once, asynchronous streams process the data incrementally, reducing the memory footprint and improving performance.
3. **Streamlined Error Handling**: Asynchronous streams allow for easier error handling using try and catch blocks within the stream processing flow.

2.2.3 Consuming Asynchronous Streams

To consume an asynchronous stream, the await keyword is used in conjunction with a foreach loop. This ensures that each item is awaited as it is retrieved.

Example:

```csharp
Copy code
public async Task ProcessNumbersAsync()
{
    await foreach (var number in GetNumbersAsync())
    {
        Console.WriteLine(number);
    }
}
```

In this example, each number is processed asynchronously as it is produced, ensuring the system remains responsive and efficient.

2.3 Exception Handling in Asynchronous Code

Handling exceptions in asynchronous code is critical for writing robust applications. In synchronous code, exceptions can be caught using try-catch blocks, and asynchronous programming follows the same principles with some additional considerations due to the nature of tasks.

2.3.1 Try-Catch with Async-Await

One of the key advantages of using async and await in C# is that exception handling is simplified. Any unhandled exceptions within an awaited task will automatically propagate back to the calling method, where they can be caught using try-catch.

Example:

```csharp
Copy code
public async Task GetDataAsync()
{
    try
    {
        var data = await DownloadDataAsync();
        Console.WriteLine(data);
    }
    catch (HttpRequestException ex)
    {
        Console.WriteLine($"Error fetching data: {ex.Message}");
    }
}
```

Here, if the DownloadDataAsync method throws an exception (e.g., due to a network failure), the exception is caught by the catch block and handled accordingly.

2.3.2 Exception Handling with Task.WhenAll

When working with multiple asynchronous operations concurrently, exception handling can become more complex. For example, when using Task.WhenAll to run multiple tasks in parallel, exceptions from any of the tasks need to be handled.

Example:

```csharp
Copy code
public async Task ProcessAllTasksAsync()
{
    var tasks = new List<Task>
    {
        Task1Async(),
        Task2Async(),
        Task3Async()
    };
```

```csharp
try
{
    await Task.WhenAll(tasks);
}
catch (Exception ex)
{
    Console.WriteLine($"An error occurred: {ex.Message}");
}
}
```

In this example, if any of the tasks in the tasks list throws an exception, it will be caught in the catch block. **Task.WhenAll** ensures that all tasks are awaited and any exceptions are handled appropriately.

2.3.3 Aggregating Exceptions

When multiple tasks throw exceptions concurrently (e.g., during a call to Task.WhenAll), the exceptions are aggregated into an **AggregateException**. Developers can inspect each individual exception to understand what went wrong in each task.

Example:

```
csharp
Copy code
try
{
    await Task.WhenAll(task1, task2, task3);
}
catch (AggregateException ae)
{
    foreach (var ex in ae.InnerExceptions)
    {
        Console.WriteLine($"Exception: {ex.Message}");
    }
}
```

The AggregateException.InnerExceptions property provides access to all exceptions that occurred during the concurrent tasks, allowing for more detailed error reporting and handling.

2.4 Advanced Task Scheduling in C#12

Task scheduling plays a critical role in optimizing the performance of asynchronous code. In C#12 and .NET 8, significant improvements have been made to the **task scheduler** to provide developers with more control over how tasks are executed.

2.4.1 The Task Scheduler

The **Task Scheduler** in .NET is responsible for queuing and executing tasks on threads. By default, tasks are executed on the **thread pool**, which automatically manages a pool of worker threads to handle multiple tasks concurrently.

In C#12, the task scheduler has been optimized for better performance, especially in high-concurrency scenarios where hundreds or thousands of tasks are being scheduled. These optimizations ensure that tasks are executed efficiently without causing thread contention or deadlocks.

2.4.2 Custom Task Scheduling

In addition to the default task scheduler, C#12 allows developers to create custom task schedulers for scenarios where more control is needed over task execution. For example, custom schedulers can be used to limit the number of concurrent tasks or to prioritize certain tasks over others.

Example:

```csharp
Copy code
public class LimitedConcurrencyTaskScheduler : TaskScheduler
{
    private readonly int _maxDegreeOfParallelism;
    private readonly List<Task> _tasks = new List<Task>();

    public LimitedConcurrencyTaskScheduler(int maxDegreeOfParallelism)
    {
        _maxDegreeOfParallelism = maxDegreeOfParallelism;
    }
```

```csharp
protected override void QueueTask(Task task)
{
    lock (_tasks)
    {
        _tasks.Add(task);
        if (_tasks.Count <= _maxDegreeOfParallelism)
        {
            ThreadPool.QueueUserWorkItem(_ =>
            TryExecuteTask(task));
        }
    }
}

protected override bool TryExecuteTaskInline(Task task, bool taskWasPreviouslyQueued)
{
    return TryExecuteTask(task);
}

protected override IEnumerable<Task> GetScheduledTasks()
{
    return _tasks;
}
}
```

This custom task scheduler limits the degree of parallelism, ensuring that only a specified number of tasks are executed concurrently. This can be useful in resource-constrained environments or when tasks must be processed in a controlled manner.

2.4.3 Using Task Schedulers in Real-World Applications

Custom task schedulers are particularly useful in systems where resource management is critical. For example, in web applications that process large numbers of simultaneous requests, limiting the number of concurrent database queries can prevent overloading the database server.

To use a custom task scheduler, pass it to the TaskFactory when creating tasks:

```csharp
Copy code
var scheduler = new LimitedConcurrencyTaskScheduler(4);
var factory = new TaskFactory(scheduler);

var tasks = new List<Task>
{
    factory.StartNew(() => Task1()),
    factory.StartNew(() => Task2()),
    factory.StartNew(() => Task3())
};

await Task.WhenAll(tasks);
```

In this example, tasks are scheduled using the custom task scheduler, which limits the number of concurrent tasks to 4.

2.5 Cancellation Tokens and Task Cancellation

Managing task cancellations is an important part of writing responsive, resource-efficient asynchronous code. In long-running or resource-intensive operations, developers need to provide mechanisms for gracefully canceling tasks.

2.5.1 Using CancellationToken

The **CancellationToken** class provides a way to signal that an asynchronous operation should be canceled. Tasks that support cancellation should take a CancellationToken parameter and periodically check whether cancellation has been requested.

Example:

```csharp
Copy code
public async Task DownloadFileAsync(string url, CancellationToken cancellationToken)
{
    using var client = new HttpClient();
    var response = await client.GetAsync(url, cancellationToken);
```

```
    var content = await response.Content.ReadAsStringAsync();
}
```

In this example, the HttpClient.GetAsync method accepts a CancellationToken, allowing the HTTP request to be canceled if necessary.

2.5.2 Checking for Cancellation

Tasks can periodically check whether cancellation has been requested by calling the IsCancellationRequested property of the CancellationToken. If cancellation is requested, the task should throw an **OperationCanceledException** to terminate the operation gracefully.

Example:

```csharp
Copy code
public async Task LongRunningTask(CancellationToken cancellationToken)
{
    for (int i = 0; i < 10; i++)
    {
        cancellationToken.ThrowIfCancellationRequested();
        await Task.Delay(1000); // Simulate work
        Console.WriteLine("Processing...");
    }
}
```

In this example, the task periodically checks for cancellation and throws an exception if cancellation is requested.

2.5.3 Cancelling Multiple Tasks

When working with multiple tasks, cancellation tokens can be used to cancel all tasks in a group. This is especially useful in scenarios where tasks are interdependent, and if one task is canceled, the others should also be stopped.

Example:

```csharp
Copy code
var cts = new CancellationTokenSource();
var token = cts.Token;

var task1 = Task1Async(token);
var task2 = Task2Async(token);

try
{
    await Task.WhenAll(task1, task2);
}
catch (OperationCanceledException)
{
    Console.WriteLine("Tasks were canceled.");
}
```

In this example, both tasks are linked to the same cancellation token, allowing them to be canceled simultaneously by calling cts.Cancel().

Conclusion

Chapter 2 explored the advanced aspects of asynchronous programming in C#12, covering critical topics like task-based asynchronous programming (TAP), asynchronous streams, exception handling, task scheduling, and task cancellation. These concepts form the foundation for writing robust, responsive, and scalable applications in C#12 and .NET 8. By mastering these techniques, developers can create high-performance systems that efficiently manage resources, handle large volumes of data, and provide a smooth, responsive user experience.

In the next chapter, we will explore **performance optimization** in asynchronous programming, including best practices for minimizing memory usage, reducing latency, and profiling asynchronous code.

Chapter 3: Performance Optimization in Asynchronous Programming with C#12

Asynchronous programming is an essential part of modern development in C#12, allowing applications to remain responsive, manage resources efficiently, and scale effectively. However, asynchronous programming comes with its own set of challenges, particularly when it comes to performance. Writing asynchronous code that not only works but is also optimized for performance is key to building scalable applications that can handle high concurrency without compromising speed or reliability.

This chapter delves into performance optimization techniques for asynchronous programming in C#12. It covers key areas such as reducing memory usage, minimizing latency, avoiding common pitfalls, and using profiling tools to measure and improve the efficiency of asynchronous code.

3.1 Understanding Performance Bottlenecks in Asynchronous Programming

Performance bottlenecks in asynchronous applications can arise from several factors. Even though asynchronous code is inherently more scalable than synchronous code, inefficient use of tasks, memory, or resources can significantly degrade performance.

3.1.1 CPU-Bound vs. I/O-Bound Operations

Before optimizing performance, it's essential to understand the nature of the tasks you are dealing with:

- **CPU-Bound Operations**: These are tasks that heavily utilize the CPU (e.g., calculations, data processing). Asynchronous programming doesn't necessarily optimize these types of tasks, since they require raw computational power. For CPU-bound tasks, multithreading and parallel processing are typically more effective than asynchronous programming.
- **I/O-Bound Operations**: These involve waiting for external resources (e.g., reading from disk, making network requests, or interacting with a database). Asynchronous programming excels at handling I/O-bound tasks, as it allows the application to remain responsive while waiting for external data.

Identifying whether a task is CPU-bound or I/O-bound is the first step in determining how to optimize its performance.

3.1.2 Common Bottlenecks in Asynchronous Programming

Several bottlenecks commonly affect the performance of asynchronous applications:

1. **Overuse of Threads**: Creating too many threads can overwhelm the system's resources, leading to thread contention and increased context switching, which decreases performance.
2. **Memory Leaks**: Asynchronous operations that are not properly handled can result in memory leaks, especially when tasks or objects are not disposed of correctly.
3. **Task Overhead**: Each asynchronous task incurs some overhead in managing the task's state and handling context switching. For lightweight tasks, the overhead of using Task or Task<T> might outweigh the benefits, leading to performance degradation.
4. **Deadlocks**: Deadlocks occur when tasks wait indefinitely for each other to complete. In asynchronous programming, deadlocks can happen if tasks are not managed properly or if blocking operations

are mixed with async code.

3.2 Reducing Memory Usage in Asynchronous Code

Memory management is a critical component of writing optimized asynchronous code. Unnecessary memory allocation and improper resource disposal can lead to bloated applications that perform poorly, especially under heavy load. In this section, we explore techniques for reducing memory consumption in asynchronous programming.

3.2.1 Using ValueTask for Performance

The **Task** object, while powerful, can introduce memory overhead, particularly in scenarios where the task completes synchronously or where tasks are frequently created and destroyed. To mitigate this overhead, C#12 offers **ValueTask**, which is a lightweight alternative to Task.

Unlike Task, which always incurs a heap allocation, ValueTask can be allocated on the stack, reducing memory pressure. This is particularly useful in high-performance applications where tasks are short-lived and frequently created.

Example:

```csharp
csharp
Copy code
public ValueTask<int> GetValueAsync()
{
    return new ValueTask<int>(42); // Synchronously completed task
}
```

In this example, ValueTask<int> is used to return a value that completes synchronously, reducing the overhead of creating a full Task<int>.

When to Use ValueTask

- Use ValueTask in scenarios where tasks are often completed synchronously or very quickly.
- Be cautious when using ValueTask, as it adds complexity to the code.

Improper use of ValueTask can lead to issues such as double-awaiting or not properly handling its lifecycle.

3.2.2 Avoiding Unnecessary Object Allocation

Frequent object allocation and garbage collection can significantly impact the performance of asynchronous applications. In particular, when tasks are created, they generate state machines that hold the task's state. Reducing unnecessary allocations is key to optimizing performance.

Optimizing with Inlining and Local Functions

Inlining asynchronous methods or using **local functions** can reduce the need for heap allocations. This is particularly helpful when small, self-contained methods are frequently called.

Example:

```csharp
Copy code
public async Task ProcessDataAsync()
{
    async Task DoWork()
    {
        await Task.Delay(100); // Simulate work
    }

    await DoWork();
}
```

Here, the DoWork method is defined locally within ProcessDataAsync. Local functions can optimize memory usage by reducing the overhead associated with method calls and task state management.

3.2.3 Efficient Use of Buffers

In applications that handle large data sets (e.g., file I/O, network streams), inefficient buffer management can lead to increased memory usage and degraded performance. Reusing buffers or leveraging buffer pools can help optimize memory usage.

The **ArrayPool<T>** class in .NET provides a way to rent and return arrays from a shared pool, reducing the number of allocations.

Example:

```csharp
Copy code
var pool = ArrayPool<byte>.Shared;
byte[] buffer = pool.Rent(1024); // Rent a 1KB buffer

try
{
    await stream.ReadAsync(buffer, 0, buffer.Length);
}
finally
{
    pool.Return(buffer); // Return the buffer to the pool
}
```

In this example, the buffer is rented from the pool and returned when no longer needed. This reduces the need for frequent allocations and deallocations of arrays, optimizing memory usage in I/O-bound tasks.

3.3 Minimizing Latency in Asynchronous Applications

Latency, or the time it takes for an operation to complete, can significantly impact the perceived performance of an asynchronous application. Minimizing latency is critical for ensuring that applications remain responsive and provide a good user experience.

3.3.1 Avoiding Blocking Calls in Async Code

One of the most common sources of latency in asynchronous applications is the use of **blocking calls**. Blocking calls cause the application to wait for a resource or task to complete, which defeats the purpose of asynchronous programming.

Avoiding Task.Result and Task.Wait

In asynchronous code, avoid using **Task.Result** or **Task.Wait**, as these methods block the calling thread until the task completes. Instead, always use await to handle asynchronous tasks.

Example:

```csharp
// Avoid
var result = myTask.Result; // Blocks the thread

// Use
var result = await myTask; // Non-blocking
```

By using await, you ensure that the calling thread remains responsive, and the operation does not cause unnecessary delays.

3.3.2 Optimizing I/O-Bound Operations

Many asynchronous tasks involve I/O-bound operations such as network requests, database queries, or file reads. These operations inherently introduce latency due to the time it takes to interact with external systems. However, there are ways to optimize these operations.

Using Buffered I/O

When performing file or network I/O, consider using **buffered I/O** to minimize the number of I/O operations and reduce latency.

Example:

```csharp
using var stream = new FileStream("file.txt", FileMode.Open, FileAccess.Read, FileShare.Read, 4096, true);
byte[] buffer = new byte[4096];
int bytesRead = await stream.ReadAsync(buffer, 0, buffer.Length);
```

Here, a buffer size of 4KB is used to read data in chunks, reducing the number of I/O operations and improving overall performance.

Batching Database Requests

When interacting with databases, consider **batching requests** to reduce round trips to the server. Instead of making multiple individual requests, group them together to minimize latency.

3.4 Best Practices for Managing Concurrency

Concurrency is at the heart of asynchronous programming. However, managing concurrency effectively is essential for ensuring that your application scales while avoiding issues like thread contention, race conditions, and deadlocks.

3.4.1 Limiting Concurrency with SemaphoreSlim

In highly concurrent applications, it's essential to control the number of tasks that run simultaneously to avoid overwhelming system resources. The **SemaphoreSlim** class provides a way to limit concurrency by restricting the number of concurrent operations.

Example:

```csharp
Copy code
private static readonly SemaphoreSlim semaphore = new SemaphoreSlim(2); // Limit to 2 concurrent tasks

public async Task ProcessTasksAsync()
{
    await semaphore.WaitAsync(); // Acquire a slot

    try
    {
        await LongRunningTask();
    }
    finally
    {
        semaphore.Release(); // Release the slot
    }
}
```

In this example, only two tasks can run concurrently. By limiting concurrency, you can prevent overloading the system and ensure that resources are used efficiently.

3.4.2 Avoiding Race Conditions in Asynchronous Code

Race conditions occur when multiple tasks attempt to modify shared data simultaneously, leading to unpredictable results. To avoid race conditions in asynchronous code, use synchronization primitives like **locks**, **mutexes**, or **concurrent collections**.

Using Locks for Synchronization

While asynchronous programming minimizes the need for locks, there are cases where shared resources must be protected.

Example:

```csharp
Copy code
private static readonly object lockObject = new object();

public void IncrementCounter()
{
    lock (lockObject)
    {
        counter++;
    }
}
```

In this example, the lock statement ensures that only one thread can access the critical section at a time, preventing race conditions.

Using Concurrent Collections

.NET provides **concurrent collections** like ConcurrentDictionary and ConcurrentQueue, which are thread-safe and ideal for scenarios where multiple tasks need to access shared data.

Example:

```csharp
Copy code
var dictionary = new ConcurrentDictionary<int, string>();

public void AddItem(int key, string value)
{
    dictionary.TryAdd(key, value);
```

}

Concurrent collections eliminate the need for manual locking, simplifying the management of shared data in highly concurrent applications.

3.5 Profiling and Measuring Asynchronous Code Performance

To effectively optimize asynchronous code, it's essential to measure performance using profiling tools. Profiling helps identify bottlenecks, inefficient code paths, and areas that consume excessive memory or CPU resources.

3.5.1 Using Visual Studio Profiler

Visual Studio includes a built-in **Profiler** that provides detailed information about the performance of your application. The profiler helps track task execution, CPU usage, memory allocation, and I/O operations.

Profiling Asynchronous Code

To profile asynchronous code in Visual Studio, follow these steps:

1. **Run the Profiler**: From the **Debug** menu, choose **Performance Profiler** and select the profiling session you want to run (e.g., CPU Usage, Memory Usage).
2. **Analyze Task Execution**: The profiler will show how long each asynchronous task takes to complete, helping you identify slow tasks or I/O bottlenecks.
3. **Track Memory Allocations**: The **Memory Usage** tool tracks how much memory is allocated and deallocated during execution. Look for tasks that allocate large amounts of memory or cause frequent garbage collection.
4. **Detect Thread Contention**: The profiler can also detect thread contention and identify tasks that block the main thread or cause unnecessary thread switching.

3.5.2 JetBrains Rider and Other Tools

In addition to Visual Studio, there are other powerful profiling tools like

JetBrains Rider, **dotTrace**, and **PerfView** that provide similar capabilities for profiling asynchronous code.

JetBrains Rider Profiling

JetBrains Rider offers built-in profiling tools that help measure CPU and memory usage, identify performance bottlenecks, and track asynchronous operations. Rider's task execution graph provides a visual representation of asynchronous code, helping developers understand task dependencies and execution order.

3.6 Handling Backpressure in Asynchronous Systems

Backpressure occurs when the system producing tasks (producer) generates work faster than the system processing tasks (consumer) can handle. In highly concurrent or real-time applications, managing backpressure is essential for maintaining system stability and performance.

3.6.1 Implementing Backpressure Control

One way to handle backpressure is to implement backpressure control mechanisms that slow down the producer when the consumer is overwhelmed. This can be done using **bounded queues** or **throttling mechanisms**.

Using Bounded Channels

The **Channel<T>** class in .NET allows you to create bounded channels that limit the number of tasks or items in the pipeline.

Example:

```csharp
Copy code
var channel = Channel.CreateBounded<int>(10); // Limit channel to 10 items

public async Task ProduceAsync()
{
    while (await channel.Writer.WaitToWriteAsync())
    {
```

```
        await channel.Writer.WriteAsync(item);
    }
}
```

In this example, the channel can hold a maximum of 10 items. If the producer generates tasks faster than the consumer can process them, the producer will wait until the consumer catches up.

Throttling API Requests

In web applications, backpressure can be managed by **throttling** API requests. This prevents the server from being overwhelmed by a flood of requests, ensuring that it remains responsive under load.

Example:

```csharp
Copy code
public async Task ThrottleRequestsAsync()
{
    await Task.Delay(500); // Add a delay between requests
    await MakeApiCallAsync();
}
```

By introducing a delay between API calls, you can control the rate at which tasks are generated and processed, reducing the risk of overwhelming the server.

Conclusion

Chapter 3 explored the critical aspects of performance optimization in asynchronous programming with C#12. We examined how to reduce memory usage using ValueTask, buffer pooling, and efficient object allocation. We also discussed minimizing latency by avoiding blocking calls, optimizing I/O operations, and managing concurrency with tools like SemaphoreSlim and concurrent collections.

Additionally, we covered how to profile asynchronous code using tools like Visual Studio's Profiler and JetBrains Rider to identify bottlenecks and inefficiencies. Lastly, we explored handling backpressure in asynchronous systems to ensure scalability and system stability under high loads.

By applying these optimization techniques, you can build responsive, efficient, and scalable asynchronous applications in C#12 and .NET 8, ensuring that your code performs well in both low- and high-concurrency environments.

Chapter 4: Best Practices for Managing Asynchronous Code in C#12

Asynchronous programming is a powerful paradigm that enables developers to create responsive and scalable applications. However, writing asynchronous code comes with its own set of challenges and pitfalls. This chapter focuses on best practices for managing asynchronous code in C#12, ensuring that developers can write efficient, maintainable, and reliable asynchronous applications.

We will cover a variety of topics, including structuring asynchronous methods, error handling, resource management, performance considerations, and testing asynchronous code. By following these best practices, you can harness the full potential of asynchronous programming while minimizing common issues.

4.1 Structuring Asynchronous Methods

The structure of asynchronous methods significantly impacts the readability, maintainability, and performance of your code. Here are some key practices for structuring asynchronous methods effectively.

4.1.1 Naming Conventions

Naming conventions play an essential role in making asynchronous code clear and understandable. When defining asynchronous methods, it is a best practice to append "Async" to the method name. This convention helps indicate that the method performs asynchronous operations.

Example:

```csharp
Copy code
public async Task<string> FetchDataAsync()
{
    // Implementation
}
```

By following this convention, you improve the clarity of your code, making it easier for others (and yourself) to understand which methods are asynchronous.

4.1.2 Method Signature

Asynchronous methods should return Task, Task<T>, or ValueTask<T> when appropriate. This allows the caller to await the method and handle its completion effectively. Ensure that asynchronous methods do not return void, as this makes error handling and flow control challenging.

Example:

```csharp
Copy code
public async Task<int> CalculateValueAsync()
{
    return await Task.FromResult(42);
}
```

If an asynchronous method is an event handler, it is acceptable to return void, but be aware of the implications for error handling in this scenario.

4.1.3 Avoiding Async Void

Avoid using async void methods, except for event handlers. async void does not provide a way to await the method, making error handling more difficult. Instead, always prefer async Task or async Task<T>.

Example:

```csharp
Copy code
// Avoid
async void OnButtonClick(object sender, EventArgs e)
{
    await PerformAsyncOperation();
}

// Use
async Task OnButtonClickAsync(object sender, EventArgs e)
{
    await PerformAsyncOperation();
}
```

By adhering to this guideline, you can ensure better control over asynchronous flow and error handling.

4.2 Error Handling in Asynchronous Code

Proper error handling is critical when working with asynchronous code. Errors can propagate differently in asynchronous contexts, and developers must implement robust mechanisms to catch and handle exceptions.

4.2.1 Try-Catch Blocks

When awaiting tasks, exceptions thrown within the awaited tasks will propagate back to the calling method. Use try-catch blocks to handle exceptions gracefully.

Example:

```csharp
Copy code
public async Task ProcessDataAsync()
{
    try
    {
```

```
            var result = await FetchDataAsync();
            Console.WriteLine(result);
        }
        catch (HttpRequestException ex)
        {
            Console.WriteLine($"Network error: {ex.Message}");
        }
        catch (Exception ex)
        {
            Console.WriteLine($"An error occurred: {ex.Message}");
        }
    }
```

In this example, different types of exceptions are caught and handled appropriately, ensuring that the application can respond to errors without crashing.

4.2.2 Using Task.WhenAll

When working with multiple asynchronous tasks, you can use Task.WhenAll to await all tasks concurrently. Be mindful that if any task fails, an AggregateException is thrown. You should handle this exception and inspect the individual task exceptions.

Example:

```
csharp
Copy code
public async Task ProcessAllAsync()
{
    var tasks = new List<Task>
    {
        Task1Async(),
        Task2Async(),
        Task3Async()
    };

    try
    {
        await Task.WhenAll(tasks);
```

```csharp
    }
    catch (AggregateException ae)
    {
        foreach (var ex in ae.InnerExceptions)
        {
            Console.WriteLine($"Task failed: {ex.Message}");
        }
    }
}
```

This approach provides a clear way to handle exceptions from multiple tasks without losing track of individual errors.

4.3 Resource Management in Asynchronous Code

Managing resources effectively is crucial in asynchronous programming. Asynchronous tasks may hold onto resources longer than expected, leading to potential resource leaks. Follow these best practices to ensure proper resource management.

4.3.1 Using Using Statements

When working with disposable resources (e.g., database connections, file streams), always use using statements to ensure proper disposal, even in asynchronous code.

Example:

```csharp
Copy code
public async Task ReadFileAsync(string filePath)
{
    using var stream = new FileStream(filePath, FileMode.Open);
    using var reader = new StreamReader(stream);
    var content = await reader.ReadToEndAsync();
    Console.WriteLine(content);
}
```

The using statement ensures that resources are disposed of correctly, preventing memory leaks.

4.3.2 Avoiding Long-Running Operations

Long-running operations should not be executed on the main thread, as they can block other tasks and degrade application performance. Instead, offload long-running operations to a separate thread or task.

Example:

```csharp
Copy code
public async Task PerformLongRunningOperationAsync()
{
    await Task.Run(() =>
    {
        // Simulate long-running work
        Thread.Sleep(5000);
    });
}
```

By using Task.Run, you can ensure that long-running operations do not block the main thread.

4.4 Best Practices for Performance Optimization

Writing asynchronous code that is performant requires careful consideration of several factors. Below are best practices that can help optimize the performance of your asynchronous applications.

4.4.1 Using ConfigureAwait

When awaiting tasks in a library or non-UI context, consider using ConfigureAwait(false). This tells the awaiter not to marshal the continuation back to the original context (e.g., the UI thread), reducing overhead and improving performance.

Example:

CHAPTER 4: BEST PRACTICES FOR MANAGING ASYNCHRONOUS CODE IN...

```csharp
Copy code
public async Task<string> GetDataAsync()
{
    var response = await
    httpClient.GetStringAsync("http://example.com").ConfigureAwait(false);
    return response;
}
```

By using ConfigureAwait(false), you can avoid unnecessary context switching, leading to performance gains.

4.4.2 Avoiding Unnecessary Async Operations

Not all methods need to be asynchronous. Evaluate whether an operation truly benefits from being asynchronous. In cases where the task is quick and doesn't involve I/O operations, a synchronous approach may be more appropriate.

Example:

```csharp
Copy code
// Avoid
public async Task<int> CalculateSumAsync(int a, int b)
{
    return await Task.FromResult(a + b); // No benefit to being
    async
}

// Use
public int CalculateSum(int a, int b)
{
    return a + b; // Synchronous is more efficient here
}
```

Evaluating the necessity of asynchronous operations can improve code clarity and performance.

4.5 Testing Asynchronous Code

Testing asynchronous code can be challenging but is crucial to ensuring the reliability of your application. Here are best practices for effectively testing asynchronous methods.

4.5.1 Unit Testing Async Methods

When writing unit tests for asynchronous methods, ensure that your test framework supports asynchronous tests. Most modern testing frameworks, such as xUnit and NUnit, allow for async test methods.

Example:

```csharp
Copy code
[Fact]
public async Task FetchDataAsync_ReturnsData()
{
    // Arrange
    var expectedData = "Hello, World!";
    var service = new DataService();

    // Act
    var result = await service.FetchDataAsync();

    // Assert
    Assert.Equal(expectedData, result);
}
```

In this example, the unit test correctly awaits the asynchronous method, ensuring that the result is validated after the operation completes.

4.5.2 Mocking Asynchronous Dependencies

When testing asynchronous methods that rely on external dependencies (e.g., HTTP clients, databases), use mocking frameworks to create stubs for those dependencies. This allows you to simulate various scenarios without relying on actual external resources.

Example using Moq:

```csharp
Copy code
var mockHttpClient = new Mock<IHttpClient>();
mockHttpClient.Setup(client =>
client.GetStringAsync(It.IsAny<string>()))
            .ReturnsAsync("Mocked Data");

var service = new DataService(mockHttpClient.Object);
var result = await service.FetchDataAsync();
```

Mocking allows you to isolate the method under test and ensure that your tests are both fast and reliable.

4.5.3 Integration Testing Asynchronous Code

In addition to unit testing, perform integration tests to validate the behavior of asynchronous methods within the context of your entire application. Ensure that all asynchronous workflows work correctly when interacting with real dependencies.

Example:

```csharp
Copy code
[Fact]
public async Task IntegrationTest_FetchDataFromApi()
{
    // Act
    var result = await realApiService.FetchDataAsync();

    // Assert
    Assert.NotNull(result);
    Assert.Contains("Expected Content", result);
}
```

Integration tests provide assurance that the asynchronous methods work correctly when interacting with actual external resources.

4.6 Conclusion

In this chapter, we covered best practices for managing asynchronous code in C#12, including structuring asynchronous methods, handling errors, managing resources, optimizing performance, and testing asynchronous code. By adhering to these best practices, developers can write efficient, maintainable, and robust asynchronous applications.

Chapter 4: Performance Optimization in Asynchronous Programming with C#12

Asynchronous programming is a powerful feature in C#12 that allows developers to write responsive, scalable applications. However, writing efficient asynchronous code requires a deep understanding of performance optimization techniques. This chapter explores various strategies for optimizing the performance of asynchronous applications in C#12, focusing on reducing latency, managing resources effectively, minimizing memory usage, and ensuring overall efficiency.

4.1 Understanding Performance in Asynchronous Applications

To effectively optimize performance, it's crucial to understand the factors that impact the performance of asynchronous applications. Performance can be influenced by various elements, including task scheduling, resource management, and how tasks interact with each other.

4.1.1 CPU-Bound vs. I/O-Bound Operations

Before diving into optimization strategies, it's essential to distinguish between CPU-bound and I/O-bound operations:

- **CPU-Bound Operations**: These tasks require significant processing power and use the CPU extensively (e.g., complex calculations, data processing). Optimizing these tasks often involves parallel processing or multithreading, rather than asynchronous programming.

- **I/O-Bound Operations**: These tasks spend most of their time waiting for external resources, such as reading from a disk or making network requests. Asynchronous programming is particularly effective in handling I/O-bound tasks, as it allows the application to remain responsive while waiting for these operations to complete.

Understanding the nature of your tasks helps determine the best optimization strategies to apply.

4.1.2 Identifying Performance Bottlenecks

Performance bottlenecks can significantly affect the responsiveness and efficiency of an application. Common bottlenecks in asynchronous applications include:

1. **Excessive Thread Usage**: Creating too many threads can lead to contention, increased context switching, and performance degradation.
2. **Memory Allocation Overhead**: Frequent allocation and deallocation of memory can lead to increased garbage collection, which negatively impacts performance.
3. **Inefficient I/O Operations**: Poorly managed I/O operations can result in excessive latency, making applications unresponsive.
4. **Task Scheduling Issues**: Inefficient task scheduling can lead to uneven distribution of workload across available threads, resulting in underutilization of resources.

Identifying these bottlenecks is crucial for optimizing performance in asynchronous applications.

4.2 Reducing Memory Usage in Asynchronous Code

Memory management is a vital aspect of optimizing asynchronous applications. Efficient memory usage not only improves performance but also reduces the likelihood of memory leaks and fragmentation. This section discusses strategies for minimizing memory usage in asynchronous code.

4.2.1 Using ValueTask for Lightweight Tasks

In C#12, the **ValueTask<T>** type offers a lightweight alternative to the

CHAPTER 4: PERFORMANCE OPTIMIZATION IN ASYNCHRONOUS...

traditional **Task<T>**. ValueTask<T> can be allocated on the stack rather than the heap, which can reduce memory overhead, particularly for short-lived or frequently completed tasks.

Example:

```csharp
Copy code
public ValueTask<int> GetDataAsync()
{
    // Return a completed ValueTask
    return new ValueTask<int>(42);
}
```

By using ValueTask<T>, you can minimize the overhead associated with heap allocations. However, be mindful of its use; improper handling can lead to complexity and potential pitfalls.

4.2.2 Object Pooling

Object pooling is a technique that allows you to reuse objects instead of creating new instances, which can significantly reduce memory allocation overhead. The **ArrayPool<T>** class in .NET provides a way to rent and return arrays from a shared pool.

Example:

```csharp
Copy code
var pool = ArrayPool<byte>.Shared;
byte[] buffer = pool.Rent(1024); // Rent a buffer

try
{
    await stream.ReadAsync(buffer, 0, buffer.Length);
}
finally
{
    pool.Return(buffer); // Return the buffer to the pool
}
```

By using object pooling, you can reduce memory allocations and improve performance, especially in scenarios where arrays are frequently created and discarded.

4.2.3 Managing Large Data Sets Efficiently

When dealing with large data sets, consider using streaming techniques to minimize memory usage. Instead of loading entire data sets into memory, process data incrementally.

Example using IAsyncEnumerable:

```csharp
Copy code
public async IAsyncEnumerable<int> GenerateNumbersAsync()
{
    for (int i = 0; i < 1000000; i++)
    {
        await Task.Delay(1); // Simulate some asynchronous work
        yield return i;
    }
}
```

By utilizing IAsyncEnumerable, you can yield data as it becomes available, reducing memory consumption and improving responsiveness.

4.3 Minimizing Latency in Asynchronous Applications

Latency, or the time it takes for an operation to complete, can significantly affect user experience. This section covers strategies to minimize latency in asynchronous applications.

4.3.1 Avoiding Blocking Calls

One of the most critical factors affecting latency is the presence of blocking calls. Avoid using synchronous calls that can block the thread, especially in asynchronous methods. Always prefer asynchronous alternatives.

Example:

```csharp
Copy code
```

```
// Avoid this
var result = myTask.Result; // Blocks the thread

// Use this
var result = await myTask; // Non-blocking
```

By using await, you allow the calling thread to remain responsive, improving the overall application performance.

4.3.2 Efficient I/O Operations

When performing I/O-bound operations, ensure you use asynchronous APIs to prevent blocking the main thread. For example, use ReadAsync and WriteAsync methods for file operations instead of their synchronous counterparts.

Example:

```
csharp
Copy code
public async Task ReadFileAsync(string filePath)
{
    using var stream = new FileStream(filePath, FileMode.Open,
    FileAccess.Read, FileShare.Read, 4096, true);
    var buffer = new byte[4096];
    int bytesRead = await stream.ReadAsync(buffer, 0,
    buffer.Length);
}
```

By utilizing asynchronous I/O operations, you can significantly reduce latency and improve the responsiveness of your application.

4.3.3 Throttling Concurrent Operations

In applications that involve multiple concurrent operations, consider implementing throttling mechanisms to limit the number of active tasks. This prevents overwhelming system resources and reduces latency during peak loads.

Example using SemaphoreSlim:

```csharp
Copy code
private static readonly SemaphoreSlim semaphore = new 
SemaphoreSlim(5); // Limit to 5 concurrent tasks

public async Task ProcessTasksAsync()
{
    await semaphore.WaitAsync();
    try
    {
        await LongRunningTask();
    }
    finally
    {
        semaphore.Release();
    }
}
```

By limiting the number of concurrent tasks, you can ensure that your application remains responsive and that resources are not exhausted.

4.4 Best Practices for Asynchronous Code Management

Managing asynchronous code effectively is crucial for maintaining the performance and reliability of applications. This section outlines best practices for writing maintainable and efficient asynchronous code.

4.4.1 Organizing Asynchronous Methods

When organizing asynchronous methods, ensure that they are logically grouped and clearly defined. Use consistent naming conventions (e.g., appending "Async" to method names) to indicate that a method performs asynchronous operations.

Example:

```csharp
Copy code
public async Task<string> FetchDataAsync()
{
    // Implementation
```

}

Organizing methods in this manner improves code readability and helps other developers understand the purpose of each method quickly.

4.4.2 Handling Cancellation Gracefully

Implement cancellation support in your asynchronous methods to allow users to cancel long-running operations. Use **CancellationToken** to signal cancellation requests.

Example:

```csharp
Copy code
public async Task<string> DownloadFileAsync(string url, 
CancellationToken cancellationToken)
{
    using var client = new HttpClient();
    return await client.GetStringAsync(url, cancellationToken);
}
```

By using cancellation tokens, you can make your application more responsive and user-friendly, especially for long-running tasks.

4.4.3 Logging and Monitoring

Implement logging and monitoring in your asynchronous code to capture important events, errors, and performance metrics. This helps in diagnosing issues and understanding application behavior in production environments.

Use libraries like **Serilog** or **NLog** to log events and performance metrics effectively.

Example:

```csharp
Copy code
public async Task<string> FetchDataAsync()
{
    try
```

```
    {
        var data = await httpClient.GetStringAsync(url);
        logger.Information("Data fetched successfully.");
        return data;
    }
    catch (Exception ex)
    {
        logger.Error($"Error fetching data: {ex.Message}");
        throw;
    }
}
```

By logging important events and errors, you can gain insights into how your asynchronous methods perform and identify areas for improvement.

4.5 Profiling Asynchronous Code for Performance Optimization

Profiling is a crucial step in optimizing performance in asynchronous applications. Profiling helps identify bottlenecks, measure resource usage, and evaluate the effectiveness of optimization strategies.

4.5.1 Using Visual Studio Profiler

Visual Studio offers a built-in profiler that allows developers to analyze the performance of their applications. It provides detailed information about CPU usage, memory allocation, and task execution.

Steps to Use the Visual Studio Profiler:

1. Open your project in Visual Studio.
2. Navigate to the **Debug** menu and select **Performance Profiler**.
3. Choose the profiling options (e.g., CPU Usage, Memory Usage).
4. Start the profiling session and interact with your application to gather performance data.

The profiler will provide insights into how your asynchronous code performs, allowing you to pinpoint areas for improvement.

4.5.2 Measuring Memory Usage

Memory usage is a critical aspect of performance optimization. Use the memory profiler to identify memory allocations, garbage collection events, and potential memory leaks in your asynchronous code.

Analyze memory snapshots to see which objects are consuming the most memory and track their lifetimes.

Example:

```csharp
Copy code
// Use a memory profiler to analyze memory usage during asynchronous operations
```

By measuring memory usage, you can make informed decisions on how to optimize your code and reduce memory overhead.

4.5.3 Identifying Task Execution Time

To evaluate the performance of asynchronous tasks, measure their execution time. Use diagnostic tools to track how long tasks take to complete and identify any performance bottlenecks.

Example:

```csharp
Copy code
var stopwatch = Stopwatch.StartNew();
await PerformTaskAsync();
stopwatch.Stop();
Console.WriteLine($"Task executed in {stopwatch.ElapsedMilliseconds} ms.");
```

By timing the execution of tasks, you can gain insights into their performance and identify slow operations that may need optimization.

4.6 Testing Asynchronous Code for Reliability

Testing asynchronous code can be challenging, but it's essential to ensure the reliability and correctness of your applications. This section covers best practices for testing asynchronous methods effectively.

4.6.1 Writing Unit Tests for Async Methods

When writing unit tests for asynchronous methods, ensure that your testing framework supports async tests. Most modern frameworks, such as

xUnit and NUnit, allow for async methods to be awaited in test cases.
Example:

```csharp
Copy code
[Fact]
public async Task FetchDataAsync_ReturnsExpectedData()
{
    var expectedData = "Hello, World!";
    var service = new DataService();

    var result = await service.FetchDataAsync();

    Assert.Equal(expectedData, result);
}
```

In this example, the async method is tested using await, ensuring that the test waits for the operation to complete before making assertions.

4.6.2 Mocking Async Dependencies

When testing asynchronous methods that rely on external services (e.g., HTTP clients, databases), use mocking frameworks to create stubs for those dependencies. This allows you to simulate various scenarios without relying on actual external resources.

Example using Moq:

```csharp
Copy code
var mockHttpClient = new Mock<IHttpClient>();
mockHttpClient.Setup(client =>
client.GetStringAsync(It.IsAny<string>()))
          .ReturnsAsync("Mocked Data");

var service = new DataService(mockHttpClient.Object);
var result = await service.FetchDataAsync();
```

By mocking dependencies, you can isolate the method under test and ensure that your tests are both fast and reliable.

4.6.3 Integration Testing Async Workflows

In addition to unit testing, perform integration tests to validate the behavior of asynchronous methods within the context of your entire application. Integration tests ensure that all asynchronous workflows work correctly when interacting with real dependencies.

Example:

```csharp
Copy code
[Fact]
public async Task IntegrationTest_FetchDataFromApi()
{
    var service = new RealApiService();

    var result = await service.FetchDataAsync();

    Assert.NotNull(result);
    Assert.Contains("Expected Content", result);
}
```

Integration tests provide assurance that the asynchronous methods work correctly when interacting with actual external resources.

Conclusion

In this chapter, we explored performance optimization techniques for asynchronous programming in C#12. We covered key areas such as understanding performance bottlenecks, reducing memory usage, minimizing latency, managing resources effectively, and testing asynchronous code for reliability.

By following the best practices outlined in this chapter, developers can write efficient, responsive, and maintainable asynchronous applications that perform well under varying loads. In the next chapter, we will delve into advanced asynchronous programming concepts, including handling complex workflows and integrating asynchronous programming with other paradigms.

Chapter 5: Advanced Techniques in Asynchronous Programming with C#12

Asynchronous programming is not just about making operations non-blocking; it also involves sophisticated patterns and techniques that can help build more responsive, efficient, and maintainable applications. In this chapter, we will explore advanced techniques for managing asynchronous operations in C#12, including combining tasks, handling concurrency, utilizing asynchronous streams, and integrating asynchronous programming with other paradigms.

5.1 Advanced Asynchronous Patterns

While the Task-based Asynchronous Pattern (TAP) provides a solid foundation for asynchronous programming, several advanced patterns can help solve more complex problems. These patterns are particularly useful in scenarios involving long-running operations, multiple dependent tasks, or complex workflows.

5.1.1 Chaining Asynchronous Operations

Chaining asynchronous operations allows developers to create workflows that depend on the completion of previous tasks. This can be achieved using the ContinueWith method, which allows you to specify a continuation task that runs after the initial task completes.

Example:

```csharp
Copy code
public Task<string> ProcessDataAsync()
{
    return FetchDataAsync().ContinueWith(fetchTask =>
    {
        // Process the fetched data
        return ProcessData(fetchTask.Result);
    });
}
```

In this example, ProcessDataAsync fetches data asynchronously and then processes it once the fetching operation is complete. The continuation task runs after the initial task, allowing you to build complex workflows without blocking the main thread.

5.1.2 Task.WhenAny

The Task.WhenAny method allows you to await multiple tasks and proceed as soon as any of them completes. This is particularly useful in scenarios where you want to take action based on the first completed task rather than waiting for all tasks to finish.

Example:

```csharp
Copy code
public async Task<string> FirstCompletedTaskAsync(IEnumerable<Task<string>> tasks)
{
    var completedTask = await Task.WhenAny(tasks);
    return await completedTask; // Return the result of the first completed task
}
```

In this example, FirstCompletedTaskAsync returns the result of the first task that completes, providing a mechanism for handling multiple tasks efficiently.

CHAPTER 5: ADVANCED TECHNIQUES IN ASYNCHRONOUS PROGRAMMING...

5.1.3 Task.WhenAll with Aggregation of Results

While Task.WhenAll is commonly used to wait for multiple tasks to complete, it can also be leveraged to aggregate results from those tasks. This is particularly useful when you need to gather data from several asynchronous operations.

Example:

```csharp
Copy code
public async Task<List<string>>
FetchAllDataAsync(IEnumerable<string> urls)
{
    var tasks = urls.Select(url => FetchDataAsync(url)).ToList();
    var results = await Task.WhenAll(tasks);
    return results.ToList(); // Aggregate results into a list
}
```

In this example, FetchAllDataAsync fetches data from multiple URLs concurrently and aggregates the results into a list, demonstrating the power of combining asynchronous tasks.

5.2 Handling Concurrency in Asynchronous Programming

Concurrency is a critical consideration in asynchronous programming, especially in applications that require the management of multiple simultaneous operations. This section discusses techniques for handling concurrency effectively in C#12.

5.2.1 Synchronization Primitives

When multiple tasks access shared resources, it's essential to manage access to those resources to avoid race conditions. C# provides several synchronization primitives that can help manage concurrency.

- **Lock**: The lock statement ensures that only one thread can access a section of code at a time.

Example:

```csharp
Copy code
private readonly object lockObject = new object();

public void IncrementCounter()
{
    lock (lockObject)
    {
        counter++;
    }
}
```

In this example, the lock statement prevents multiple threads from incrementing the counter simultaneously, ensuring thread-safe access to shared resources.

- **SemaphoreSlim**: The SemaphoreSlim class is a lightweight synchronization primitive that limits the number of threads that can access a resource concurrently.

Example:

```csharp
Copy code
private static readonly SemaphoreSlim semaphore = new SemaphoreSlim(2); // Limit to 2 concurrent threads

public async Task AccessResourceAsync()
{
    await semaphore.WaitAsync();
    try
    {
        // Access shared resource
    }
    finally
    {
        semaphore.Release();
```

CHAPTER 5: ADVANCED TECHNIQUES IN ASYNCHRONOUS PROGRAMMING...

    }
}

In this example, SemaphoreSlim is used to limit access to a shared resource to two concurrent threads, ensuring that resources are managed effectively.

5.2.2 Avoiding Deadlocks

Deadlocks occur when two or more tasks are waiting for each other to complete, resulting in a standstill. To avoid deadlocks in asynchronous programming:

1. **Avoid Blocking Calls**: Ensure that your asynchronous methods do not block the main thread by using await instead of blocking methods.
2. **Use Timeout**: When waiting for a resource, consider using timeouts to prevent indefinite blocking.
3. **Consistent Lock Ordering**: If multiple locks are required, establish a consistent order in which locks are acquired to prevent circular dependencies.

Example of Avoiding Deadlocks:

```csharp
Copy code
public async Task MethodAAsync()
{
    await semaphore.WaitAsync();
    try
    {
        await MethodBAsync(); // Avoid calling synchronously
    }
    finally
    {
        semaphore.Release();
    }
}
```

```
public async Task MethodBAsync()
{
    await semaphore.WaitAsync();
    try
    {
        // Resource access
    }
    finally
    {
        semaphore.Release();
    }
}
```

By ensuring that tasks do not call each other synchronously, you can prevent deadlocks from occurring.

5.3 Working with Asynchronous Streams in C#12

Asynchronous streams provide a powerful mechanism for handling streams of data in a non-blocking way. C#12 enhances the capabilities of asynchronous streams, making it easier to work with data that is produced over time.

5.3.1 Introduction to IAsyncEnumerable

The IAsyncEnumerable<T> interface allows you to represent a collection of data that can be iterated over asynchronously. This is particularly useful for scenarios where data is fetched incrementally, such as reading from a network source or processing large files.

Example:

```csharp
Copy code
public async IAsyncEnumerable<int> GenerateNumbersAsync()
{
    for (int i = 0; i < 100; i++)
    {
        await Task.Delay(100); // Simulate asynchronous work
        yield return i; // Return numbers asynchronously
    }
```

```
}
```

In this example, the GenerateNumbersAsync method produces numbers asynchronously, allowing consumers to iterate over the data as it becomes available.

5.3.2 Consuming Asynchronous Streams

To consume asynchronous streams, use the await foreach construct, which allows you to iterate over IAsyncEnumerable<T> without blocking.

Example:

```csharp
Copy code
public async Task ProcessNumbersAsync()
{
    await foreach (var number in GenerateNumbersAsync())
    {
        Console.WriteLine(number);
    }
}
```

By using await foreach, you can process each item in the stream as it is produced, maintaining responsiveness in your application.

5.3.3 Combining Asynchronous Streams

Asynchronous streams can be combined and transformed using LINQ-like methods. This allows you to build complex data pipelines that process data incrementally.

Example:

```csharp
Copy code
public async IAsyncEnumerable<int> FilterEvenNumbersAsync()
{
    await foreach (var number in GenerateNumbersAsync())
    {
        if (number % 2 == 0)
```

```
        {
            yield return number; // Only yield even numbers
        }
    }
}
```

In this example, the FilterEvenNumbersAsync method filters out odd numbers from the generated sequence, demonstrating how to build a pipeline with asynchronous streams.

5.4 Integrating Asynchronous Programming with Other Paradigms

Asynchronous programming often needs to be integrated with other programming paradigms, such as functional programming and reactive programming. Understanding how to blend these paradigms can lead to more robust and maintainable code.

5.4.1 Functional Programming with Asynchronous Code

Functional programming emphasizes immutability and pure functions, which can lead to clearer and more predictable asynchronous code. When working with asynchronous methods, consider the following functional programming principles:

- **Use Pure Functions**: Design your asynchronous methods as pure functions that produce the same output for the same input without side effects.
- **Higher-Order Functions**: Create higher-order functions that take other functions as parameters or return them as results. This allows for flexible and composable asynchronous operations.

Example:

```csharp
Copy code
public Func<string, Task<string>> FetchData = async (url) =>
{
```

CHAPTER 5: ADVANCED TECHNIQUES IN ASYNCHRONOUS PROGRAMMING...

```csharp
    using var client = new HttpClient();
    return await client.GetStringAsync(url);
};
```

In this example, FetchData is a higher-order function that returns a task for fetching data, allowing for flexible usage.

5.4.2 Reactive Programming with Asynchronous Streams

Reactive programming focuses on building applications that react to changes in data or events. Asynchronous streams can be a powerful tool for implementing reactive patterns in C#12.

Using libraries like **Reactive Extensions (Rx)**, you can create observables that emit values over time and respond to those values with asynchronous operations.

Example using Rx:

```
csharp
Copy code
var observable = Observable.Create<string>(observer =>
{
    observer.OnNext("Data 1");
    observer.OnNext("Data 2");
    observer.OnCompleted();
    return Disposable.Empty;
});

observable.Subscribe(
    data => Console.WriteLine(data),
    ex => Console.WriteLine($"Error: {ex.Message}"),
    () => Console.WriteLine("Completed"));
```

In this example, an observable emits data asynchronously, demonstrating how to integrate reactive programming principles with asynchronous programming in C#12.

5.5 Profiling and Measuring Asynchronous Performance

To ensure that your asynchronous applications perform optimally, it's essential to profile and measure their performance continuously. Profiling allows you to identify bottlenecks and optimize the application's performance based on actual usage patterns.

5.5.1 Profiling Tools in Visual Studio

Visual Studio provides a built-in profiler that allows developers to analyze the performance of their asynchronous applications. The profiler can measure CPU usage, memory allocations, and task execution times.

Steps to Profile Asynchronous Applications:

1. **Open the Performance Profiler**: From the **Debug** menu, select **Performance Profiler**.
2. **Choose Profiling Tools**: Select the profiling tools you want to use (e.g., CPU Usage, Memory Usage).
3. **Run Your Application**: Start profiling your application and interact with it to gather performance data.
4. **Analyze Results**: After profiling, analyze the results to identify performance bottlenecks and areas for improvement.
5. **5.2 Analyzing Task Execution and Memory Usage**

When analyzing your application's performance, pay close attention to:

- **Task Execution Time**: Measure how long individual tasks take to complete. This information can help identify slow operations that need optimization.
- **Memory Allocations**: Use memory profiling to track memory allocations during asynchronous operations. Look for excessive allocations or memory leaks that can degrade performance.

Example of Timing Execution:

```
csharp
Copy code
var stopwatch = Stopwatch.StartNew();
await PerformAsyncOperation();
```

```
stopwatch.Stop();
Console.WriteLine($"Operation completed in 
{stopwatch.ElapsedMilliseconds} ms.");
```

By measuring task execution times and analyzing memory usage, you can make informed decisions on how to optimize your asynchronous code.

5.5.3 Continuous Monitoring in Production

In production environments, continuously monitoring the performance of your asynchronous applications is crucial. Use application performance monitoring (APM) tools like **Application Insights** or **New Relic** to track metrics such as response times, error rates, and resource utilization.

These tools can provide real-time insights into how your application performs under load, allowing you to make proactive adjustments and optimizations as needed.

Conclusion

Chapter 5 explored advanced techniques in asynchronous programming with C#12, covering a range of topics from complex patterns to concurrency management and integration with other paradigms. By mastering these techniques, developers can write more efficient, responsive, and maintainable asynchronous applications.

In this chapter, we discussed:

- Advanced asynchronous patterns, including chaining operations and handling multiple tasks.
- Techniques for managing concurrency effectively and avoiding common pitfalls.
- The benefits of asynchronous streams and how to utilize them for incremental data processing.
- Integration of asynchronous programming with functional and reactive programming paradigms.
- Profiling and measuring performance to identify bottlenecks and

optimize resource usage.

Armed with these advanced techniques and best practices, you are now better equipped to harness the power of asynchronous programming in C#12 to build high-performance applications. In the next chapter, we will delve into testing strategies for asynchronous code, ensuring that your applications are robust and reliable.

Chapter 6: Testing Asynchronous Code in C#12

As applications become more complex and increasingly reliant on asynchronous programming, ensuring the reliability and correctness of asynchronous code is paramount. Testing asynchronous code requires a different approach than traditional synchronous code due to its non-blocking nature and potential complexities. In this chapter, we will explore the best practices and techniques for effectively testing asynchronous methods in C#12, ensuring that your applications function as expected under various scenarios.

6.1 Understanding the Challenges of Testing Asynchronous Code

Testing asynchronous code introduces unique challenges that developers must navigate. Understanding these challenges is the first step in developing effective testing strategies.

6.1.1 Timing Issues

Asynchronous operations may not complete in a predictable order, leading to timing-related issues. This unpredictability can make it difficult to assert the state of the application or the results of asynchronous operations.

Example:

```csharp
Copy code
var result = await asyncOperation(); // Timing issue: result might not be ready
Assert.IsTrue(result); // This may fail if the operation hasn't completed yet
```

Testing frameworks typically execute assertions before the asynchronous operation completes, leading to potential failures.

6.1.2 Exception Handling

Exceptions thrown during asynchronous operations behave differently than synchronous exceptions. When a task is awaited, any exceptions that occur within that task are propagated back to the calling context. However, if the task is not awaited, unhandled exceptions may lead to application crashes.

Example:

```csharp
Copy code
public async Task FaultyMethodAsync()
{
    throw new InvalidOperationException("An error occurred!");
}

// This will not capture the exception
FaultyMethodAsync(); // No await
```

Properly capturing and handling exceptions in asynchronous tests is crucial for ensuring that tests behave as expected.

6.1.3 Dependency Management

Asynchronous methods often depend on external resources, such as databases, web services, or file systems. These dependencies can introduce variability in tests, making it challenging to create reliable, deterministic tests.

Example:

```csharp
Copy code
public async Task<string> FetchDataAsync()
{
    // Call an external service
    return await
    httpClient.GetStringAsync("https://api.example.com/data");
}
```

To create stable tests, developers must mock or simulate these dependencies.

6.2 Unit Testing Asynchronous Methods

Unit testing asynchronous methods is essential for ensuring that individual components function correctly. This section covers best practices for writing unit tests for asynchronous code.

6.2.1 Using Testing Frameworks

Modern testing frameworks, such as xUnit and NUnit, provide excellent support for testing asynchronous code. These frameworks allow you to define asynchronous test methods using the async keyword and await asynchronous operations.

Example using xUnit:

```csharp
Copy code
[Fact]
public async Task FetchDataAsync_ReturnsExpectedData()
{
    var service = new DataService();
    var expectedData = "Hello, World!";

    var result = await service.FetchDataAsync();

    Assert.Equal(expectedData, result);
}
```

In this example, the asynchronous test method is defined using async, and the asynchronous operation is awaited, ensuring that the test runs correctly.

6.2.2 Setting Up Mocked Dependencies

To test asynchronous methods that depend on external services, use mocking frameworks like **Moq** or **NSubstitute** to create mock objects. This allows you to simulate the behavior of external dependencies and isolate the method under test.

Example using Moq:

```csharp
Copy code
var mockHttpClient = new Mock<IHttpClient>();
mockHttpClient.Setup(client =>
client.GetStringAsync(It.IsAny<string>()))
            .ReturnsAsync("Mocked Data");

var service = new DataService(mockHttpClient.Object);
var result = await service.FetchDataAsync();

Assert.Equal("Mocked Data", result);
```

In this example, the mocked IHttpClient returns a predefined response, allowing you to test the FetchDataAsync method without relying on an actual HTTP request.

6.2.3 Testing Task Completion and Timing

When testing asynchronous methods, you may need to assert that a task has completed or measure the time it takes to complete a task. Use the Task class to check the status of tasks and ensure they are awaited properly.

Example of Task Completion:

```csharp
Copy code
public async Task ProcessDataAsync()
{
    var task = PerformAsyncOperation();
    Assert.False(task.IsCompleted); // Task should not be
```

```
completed yet
await task; // Await the task
Assert.True(task.IsCompleted); // Verify that the task is
completed
}
```

By checking the task's completion status, you can ensure that the asynchronous operations are functioning as expected.

6.3 Handling Exceptions in Asynchronous Tests

Properly handling exceptions in asynchronous tests is essential for ensuring that your tests behave as expected. This section discusses strategies for capturing and asserting exceptions in asynchronous methods.

6.3.1 Using Assert.ThrowsAsync

To assert that an exception is thrown in an asynchronous method, use the Assert.ThrowsAsync method provided by testing frameworks. This method allows you to specify the type of exception you expect and await the asynchronous operation.

Example:

```csharp
Copy code
[Fact]
public async Task FetchDataAsync_ThrowsException_WhenInvalidUrl()
{
    var service = new DataService();

    await Assert.ThrowsAsync<InvalidOperationException>(async () =>
    {
        await service.FetchDataAsync("invalid-url");
    });
}
```

In this example, the test asserts that FetchDataAsync throws an InvalidOperationException when given an invalid URL.

6.3.2 Verifying Exception Messages

You can also verify the exception message to ensure that the correct exception is thrown with the expected message. After asserting the exception, you can inspect its properties.

Example:

```csharp
Copy code
[Fact]
public async Task FetchDataAsync_ThrowsException_WithExpectedMessage()
{
    var service = new DataService();

    var exception = await Assert.ThrowsAsync<InvalidOperationException>(async () =>
    {
        await service.FetchDataAsync("invalid-url");
    });

    Assert.Equal("An error occurred while fetching data.", exception.Message);
}
```

This example demonstrates how to assert both the type of the exception and its message, ensuring that the error handling in your asynchronous methods is functioning correctly.

6.4 Integration Testing Asynchronous Workflows

Integration testing is crucial for ensuring that asynchronous methods work correctly in the context of the entire application. This section discusses best practices for writing integration tests for asynchronous workflows.

6.4.1 Setting Up the Integration Test Environment

When performing integration tests, ensure that your test environment is configured to use real dependencies, such as databases, message queues, or external services. This allows you to validate the end-to-end behavior of your asynchronous workflows.

Example of Setting Up an Integration Test:

```csharp
Copy code
public class IntegrationTests : IClassFixture<DatabaseFixture>
{
    private readonly DatabaseFixture _fixture;

    public IntegrationTests(DatabaseFixture fixture)
    {
        _fixture = fixture;
    }

    [Fact]
    public async Task ProcessDataAsync_SavesDataCorrectly()
    {
        var service = new DataService(_fixture.DbContext);

        await service.ProcessDataAsync();

        var data = await
_fixture.DbContext.DataRecords.FirstOrDefaultAsync();
        Assert.NotNull(data);
        Assert.Equal("Expected Value", data.Value);
    }
}
```

In this example, the integration test verifies that the ProcessDataAsync method correctly saves data to the database by using a shared DatabaseFixture to set up the database context.

6.4.2 Testing Asynchronous Event Handlers

Integration tests are also useful for verifying the behavior of asynchronous event handlers. When an event is triggered, the corresponding asynchronous method should respond correctly.

Example:

```csharp
Copy code
[Fact]
public async Task HandleEventAsync_ProcessesDataCorrectly()
{
    var service = new EventService();
    var handler = new EventHandler(service);

    await handler.HandleAsync(new EventData { /* Event data */ });

    var result = await service.GetProcessedDataAsync();
    Assert.Equal("Expected Result", result);
}
```

In this example, the integration test checks that the event handler processes the data correctly when the event is triggered.

6.5 Mocking Asynchronous Dependencies

Mocking external dependencies is essential for isolating tests and ensuring that they run reliably. This section discusses how to effectively mock asynchronous dependencies in your tests.

6.5.1 Using Moq for Mocking

The **Moq** framework is a popular choice for creating mock objects in C#. Moq allows you to set up expectations and simulate the behavior of dependencies, including asynchronous methods.

Example of Mocking Asynchronous Dependencies:

```csharp
Copy code
var mockService = new Mock<IDataService>();
mockService.Setup(service =>
service.GetDataAsync()).ReturnsAsync("Mocked Data");

var consumer = new Consumer(mockService.Object);
var result = await consumer.ProcessDataAsync();

Assert.Equal("Processed: Mocked Data", result);
```

In this example, the mocked IDataService simulates the behavior of an asynchronous method, allowing you to test the Consumer class without relying on actual data fetching.

6.5.2 Verifying Interaction with Mocks

You can also verify that your code interacts correctly with mocked dependencies by asserting that specific methods are called with the expected parameters.

Example of Verifying Method Calls:

```csharp
Copy code
mockService.Verify(service => service.GetDataAsync(), Times.Once);
```

This assertion checks that the GetDataAsync method was called exactly once during the test, ensuring that your code interacts with dependencies as expected.

6.6 Continuous Testing in Asynchronous Development

In modern software development, continuous testing is crucial for maintaining code quality. Asynchronous code is no exception. This section discusses strategies for implementing continuous testing practices for asynchronous applications.

6.6.1 Automated Testing Pipelines

Set up automated testing pipelines using continuous integration (CI) tools like **GitHub Actions**, **Azure DevOps**, or **Jenkins**. These tools can automatically run your test suite whenever code is pushed to the repository, ensuring that your asynchronous code remains reliable.

Example of a CI Pipeline:

```yaml
Copy code
# GitHub Actions example
name: CI
```

```yaml
on:
  push:
    branches:
      - main

jobs:
  test:
    runs-on: ubuntu-latest
    steps:
      - uses: actions/checkout@v2
      - name: Set up .NET
        uses: actions/setup-dotnet@v1
        with:
          dotnet-version: '6.0.x'
      - name: Restore dependencies
        run: dotnet restore
      - name: Run tests
        run: dotnet test
```

This pipeline ensures that tests are run automatically, providing immediate feedback on code changes and catching issues early.

6.6.2 Test Coverage Analysis

Incorporate test coverage analysis tools to evaluate how much of your asynchronous code is covered by tests. Tools like **coverlet** and **dotCover** can help identify untested code paths and ensure comprehensive test coverage.

Example of Running Coverage Analysis:

```bash
Copy code
dotnet test --collect:"XPlat Code Coverage"
```

This command runs the tests and collects code coverage data, allowing you to assess the effectiveness of your testing strategy.

Conclusion

In this chapter, we explored the complexities of testing asynchronous code in C#12. We covered the challenges associated with testing asynchronous methods, including timing issues, exception handling, and dependency management. Best practices for unit testing asynchronous code were discussed, along with strategies for integration testing, mocking asynchronous dependencies, and implementing continuous testing practices.

By following the guidelines and techniques outlined in this chapter, you can ensure that your asynchronous code is thoroughly tested, reliable, and maintainable. Testing is a critical part of the development process, and with the right approach, you can confidently build robust asynchronous applications that perform well in real-world scenarios.

In the next chapter, we will delve into **real-world scenarios and case studies**, illustrating how to apply asynchronous programming techniques to solve practical problems in C#12 applications.

Chapter 7: Best Practices for Designing Asynchronous APIs in C#12

Designing asynchronous APIs is essential for creating responsive, efficient applications in C#12. As more applications adopt asynchronous programming models, it's crucial to follow best practices that promote clean, maintainable, and user-friendly asynchronous APIs. This chapter will explore various strategies for designing effective asynchronous APIs, covering method signatures, exception handling, documentation, and user experience.

7.1 Understanding Asynchronous API Design Principles

Before diving into specific practices, it's important to grasp the fundamental principles that underpin good asynchronous API design.

7.1.1 Clarity and Simplicity

An asynchronous API should be clear and straightforward to use. Developers should be able to understand how to interact with the API without extensive documentation. Use intuitive naming conventions and method signatures that reflect the asynchronous nature of operations.

Example:

```csharp
Copy code
public async Task<string> GetDataAsync(); // Clear and descriptive
```

By following clear naming conventions, you enhance the readability of your API, making it easier for other developers to adopt and use.

7.1.2 Consistency

Consistency is key in API design. Asynchronous methods should follow a uniform pattern throughout your API, including naming conventions, return types, and exception handling mechanisms. This consistency helps developers build a mental model of how to use the API effectively.

Example: All asynchronous methods in your API should end with "Async" and return Task or Task<T>:

```csharp
Copy code
public async Task<bool> SaveDataAsync(DataModel data);
public async Task<List<DataModel>> FetchDataAsync();
```

Establishing consistent patterns improves usability and reduces cognitive load for developers.

7.1.3 Usability

The usability of an API is crucial for its adoption. Ensure that your asynchronous methods are easy to call and integrate with existing code. Provide meaningful default values, sensible overloads, and well-thought-out parameters.

Example:

```csharp
Copy code
public async Task<string> FetchDataAsync(string url, 
CancellationToken cancellationToken = default);
```

By providing optional parameters with sensible defaults, you enhance usability and allow developers to call methods without excessive configuration.

7.2 Designing Asynchronous Method Signatures

Method signatures are a fundamental aspect of asynchronous API design. This section discusses best practices for defining asynchronous method signatures in C#12.

7.2.1 Returning Task vs. Task<T>

Decide whether to return a Task or Task<T> based on the purpose of the method. If the method performs an operation without returning a value, use Task. If the method computes a result, use Task<T>.

Example:

```csharp
Copy code
public async Task SaveDataAsync(DataModel data); // No return value
public async Task<List<DataModel>> FetchDataAsync(); // Returns a list of data
```

By choosing the appropriate return type, you provide clear expectations for how the method should be used.

7.2.2 Avoiding Async Void

Avoid returning void from asynchronous methods unless they are event handlers. async void methods do not provide a way to await them, making error handling more challenging.

Example:

```csharp
Copy code
// Avoid
public async void OnButtonClick(object sender, EventArgs e)
{
    await DoWorkAsync();
}

// Use
```

```csharp
public async Task OnButtonClickAsync(object sender, EventArgs e)
{
    await DoWorkAsync();
}
```

Returning Task from asynchronous methods enables better error handling and flow control.

7.2.3 Use of Cancellation Tokens

Asynchronous methods should accept a CancellationToken parameter to allow callers to cancel long-running operations. This is especially important for methods that involve I/O-bound tasks or long computations.

Example:

```csharp
Copy code
public async Task<string> FetchDataAsync(string url, 
CancellationToken cancellationToken);
```

By incorporating cancellation tokens, you improve the flexibility and responsiveness of your API.

7.3 Exception Handling in Asynchronous APIs

Robust exception handling is critical for maintaining the reliability of asynchronous APIs. This section discusses strategies for handling exceptions effectively.

7.3.1 Propagating Exceptions

Asynchronous methods should propagate exceptions naturally to the caller. When an asynchronous operation fails, the exception should be thrown when the task is awaited. This allows callers to handle exceptions using standard try-catch constructs.

Example:

```csharp
Copy code
```

```csharp
public async Task<string> FetchDataAsync(string url)
{
    using var client = new HttpClient();
    return await client.GetStringAsync(url); // Exception will be
    propagated
}
```

By propagating exceptions, you provide a predictable way for callers to handle errors.

7.3.2 Providing Meaningful Exception Messages

When throwing exceptions from asynchronous methods, ensure that the messages are meaningful and informative. This helps developers understand the cause of the error and how to resolve it.

Example:

```
csharp
Copy code
throw new InvalidOperationException("Failed to fetch data from
the provided URL.");
```

Meaningful exception messages improve the developer experience and assist in troubleshooting.

7.3.3 Documenting Exceptions

Document the exceptions that can be thrown by your asynchronous methods. This documentation should include both the types of exceptions and the conditions under which they may occur.

Example:

```
csharp
Copy code
/// <summary>
/// Fetches data from the specified URL.
/// </summary>
/// <param name="url">The URL to fetch data from.</param>
/// <param name="cancellationToken">Cancellation token.</param>
```

CHAPTER 7: BEST PRACTICES FOR DESIGNING ASYNCHRONOUS APIS IN...

```
/// <returns>Task that represents the asynchronous
operation.</returns>
/// <exception cref="HttpRequestException">Thrown when an error
occurs while fetching data.</exception>
/// <exception cref="InvalidOperationException">Thrown when the
URL is invalid.</exception>
public async Task<string> FetchDataAsync(string url,
CancellationToken cancellationToken);
```

By documenting exceptions, you provide clear expectations for users of your API.

7.4 Documentation and Usability of Asynchronous APIs

Good documentation is essential for ensuring that developers can use your asynchronous APIs effectively. This section covers best practices for documenting asynchronous methods.

7.4.1 Clear and Concise Documentation

Provide clear, concise documentation for each asynchronous method, including the purpose of the method, its parameters, return values, and any exceptions it may throw. This information helps developers understand how to use the API correctly.

Example:

```csharp
Copy code
/// <summary>
/// Saves the specified data asynchronously.
/// </summary>
/// <param name="data">The data model to save.</param>
/// <returns>A task that represents the asynchronous
operation.</returns>
/// <exception cref="InvalidOperationException">Thrown when the
data is invalid.</exception>
public async Task SaveDataAsync(DataModel data);
```

By documenting asynchronous methods thoroughly, you improve usability and reduce the likelihood of misuse.

7.4.2 Code Examples

Include code examples in the documentation to demonstrate how to use asynchronous methods. Practical examples help developers understand the intended usage and provide a quick reference for implementation.

Example:

```csharp
Copy code
// Example usage of FetchDataAsync
var dataService = new DataService();
try
{
    var data = await
    dataService.FetchDataAsync("https://api.example.com/data");
    Console.WriteLine(data);
}
catch (HttpRequestException ex)
{
    Console.WriteLine($"Error fetching data: {ex.Message}");
}
```

Providing code examples in documentation enhances clarity and usability.

7.5 User Experience Considerations

Designing asynchronous APIs is not just about the code; it also involves considering the user experience. This section discusses how to enhance the user experience when interacting with asynchronous APIs.

7.5.1 Progress Indicators

For long-running asynchronous operations, consider providing progress indicators or feedback mechanisms to inform users about the status of the operation. This is especially important in user-facing applications.

Example:

```csharp
Copy code
public async Task ProcessDataWithProgressAsync(IProgress<int> progress)
```

```csharp
{
    for (int i = 0; i <= 100; i++)
    {
        await Task.Delay(100); // Simulate work
        progress.Report(i); // Report progress
    }
}
```

By implementing progress reporting, you can enhance the user experience and keep users informed about ongoing operations.

7.5.2 Providing Async-First APIs

When designing new APIs, consider making them asynchronous from the outset. By providing asynchronous versions of methods as the primary API, you enable developers to leverage asynchronous programming without relying on synchronous alternatives.

Example:

```
csharp
Copy code
public async Task<DataModel> GetDataAsync(); // Primary method
public DataModel GetData();  // Optional synchronous method
```

By prioritizing asynchronous methods, you encourage best practices and promote a responsive design.

7.6 Summary

In this chapter, we explored best practices for designing asynchronous APIs in C#12. We covered several critical aspects, including:

- The importance of clarity, simplicity, and consistency in API design.
- Strategies for defining asynchronous method signatures, including returning Task or Task<T> and handling cancellation.
- Best practices for exception handling, including propagating exceptions and providing meaningful messages.

- The significance of clear documentation and usability, including code examples and progress indicators.
- User experience considerations that enhance the usability of asynchronous APIs.

By adhering to these best practices, developers can create asynchronous APIs that are intuitive, reliable, and efficient, allowing other developers to leverage the power of asynchronous programming in their applications. In the next chapter, we will explore performance tuning and optimization techniques specific to asynchronous applications in C#12.

Chapter 8: Real-World Scenarios and Case Studies in Asynchronous Programming with C#12

Asynchronous programming is increasingly being adopted in real-world applications due to its ability to enhance responsiveness and performance. In this chapter, we will explore several real-world scenarios and case studies that illustrate the practical use of asynchronous programming techniques in C#12. These examples will cover various domains, including web applications, desktop applications, data processing, and more.

8.1 Scenario 1: Building a Responsive Web API

In today's fast-paced web environment, responsiveness is crucial. Users expect applications to load quickly and provide real-time data updates. This section explores how to build a responsive web API using asynchronous programming in C#12.

8.1.1 Designing the API

Suppose we are building an online bookstore API that provides access to book information, orders, and user accounts. The API will need to handle a variety of asynchronous operations, such as fetching data from a database, processing orders, and interacting with third-party services for payment processing.

Example of an Asynchronous Controller:

```csharp
Copy code
[ApiController]
[Route("api/[controller]")]
public class BooksController : ControllerBase
{
    private readonly IBookService _bookService;

    public BooksController(IBookService bookService)
    {
        _bookService = bookService;
    }

    [HttpGet("{id}")]
    public async Task<ActionResult<Book>> GetBookAsync(int id)
    {
        var book = await _bookService.GetBookByIdAsync(id);
        if (book == null)
        {
            return NotFound();
        }
        return Ok(book);
    }
}
```

In this example, the GetBookAsync method retrieves book information asynchronously. By using async and await, the method remains non-blocking, allowing the API to handle other requests while waiting for the database operation to complete.

8.1.2 Fetching Data Asynchronously

When fetching data, we can optimize the performance of our API by implementing asynchronous data access. Suppose we are using Entity Framework Core to interact with the database.

Example of an Asynchronous Service Method:

```csharp
Copy code
public class BookService : IBookService
{
    private readonly BookDbContext _context;

    public BookService(BookDbContext context)
    {
        _context = context;
    }

    public async Task<Book> GetBookByIdAsync(int id)
    {
        return await _context.Books.FindAsync(id);
    }
}
```

Here, the GetBookByIdAsync method uses the FindAsync method provided by Entity Framework Core, allowing it to fetch data asynchronously. This ensures that the database operation does not block the thread, enabling better scalability.

8.1.3 Handling Concurrency in Web APIs

In a web API, multiple clients may attempt to access or modify the same data simultaneously. Properly handling concurrency is essential to prevent data corruption.

Example of Optimistic Concurrency Control:

```csharp
Copy code
public async Task<ActionResult<Book>> UpdateBookAsync(int id, Book updatedBook)
{
    if (id != updatedBook.Id)
    {
        return BadRequest();
    }
```

```csharp
    _context.Entry(updatedBook).State = EntityState.Modified;

    try
    {
        await _context.SaveChangesAsync();
    }
    catch (DbUpdateConcurrencyException)
    {
        if (!BookExists(id))
        {
            return NotFound();
        }
        else
        {
            throw; // Re-throw the exception for further handling
        }
    }

    return NoContent();
}
```

In this example, the UpdateBookAsync method handles potential concurrency conflicts by catching DbUpdateConcurrencyException. If the record has been modified by another client, the API can respond appropriately, ensuring data integrity.

8.2 Scenario 2: Building a Desktop Application with Asynchronous I/O

Desktop applications often require interaction with files, databases, or remote services. Ensuring responsiveness during these operations is critical. This section explores how to implement asynchronous I/O in a C# desktop application.

8.2.1 Creating a Responsive UI

When building a Windows Forms or WPF application, long-running operations (like file loading or network requests) should be performed asynchronously to keep the UI responsive.

Example of Asynchronous File Loading:

```csharp
Copy code
private async void LoadDataButton_Click(object sender, EventArgs e)
{
    var data = await LoadDataAsync();
    UpdateUI(data);
}

private async Task<List<string>> LoadDataAsync()
{
    using var reader = new StreamReader("data.txt");
    var content = await reader.ReadToEndAsync();
    return content.Split('\n').ToList();
}
```

In this example, the LoadDataButton_Click event handler calls LoadDataAsync, which reads data from a file asynchronously. The UI remains responsive while the data is being loaded.

8.2.2 Handling User Cancellation

In a desktop application, users may want to cancel long-running operations. Implementing cancellation support is essential for providing a good user experience.

Example of Using Cancellation Tokens:

```csharp
Copy code
private CancellationTokenSource _cancellationTokenSource;

private async void LoadDataButton_Click(object sender, EventArgs e)
{
    _cancellationTokenSource = new CancellationTokenSource();
    var token = _cancellationTokenSource.Token;

    try
    {
        var data = await LoadDataAsync(token);
```

```
        UpdateUI(data);
    }
    catch (OperationCanceledException)
    {
        MessageBox.Show("Loading canceled.");
    }
}

private async Task<List<string>> LoadDataAsync(CancellationToken
cancellationToken)
{
    using var reader = new StreamReader("data.txt");
    var content = await reader.ReadToEndAsync(cancellationToken);
    return content.Split('\n').ToList();
}

// Cancellation handler
private void CancelButton_Click(object sender, EventArgs e)
{
    _cancellationTokenSource?.Cancel();
}
```

In this example, the application allows users to cancel the loading operation by clicking the "Cancel" button. The CancellationToken is passed to the asynchronous method, enabling cancellation handling.

8.3 Scenario 3: Data Processing Pipeline

Asynchronous programming is ideal for building data processing pipelines, where data is transformed and processed in stages. This section explores how to create an asynchronous data processing pipeline.

8.3.1 Designing the Pipeline

Suppose we are developing an application that processes user-uploaded images. The pipeline will include stages for validating the images, resizing them, and saving them to a database.

Example of an Asynchronous Processing Pipeline:

CHAPTER 8: REAL-WORLD SCENARIOS AND CASE STUDIES IN...

```csharp
Copy code
public async Task ProcessImagesAsync(IEnumerable<string> imagePaths)
{
    foreach (var path in imagePaths)
    {
        var image = await LoadImageAsync(path);
        var resizedImage = ResizeImage(image);
        await SaveImageToDatabaseAsync(resizedImage);
    }
}
```

In this example, the ProcessImagesAsync method processes a collection of image paths. Each image is loaded asynchronously, resized synchronously (assuming it's a quick operation), and then saved to the database asynchronously.

8.3.2 Implementing Parallel Processing

To improve throughput, consider processing images in parallel. This can be achieved using Task.WhenAll to run multiple asynchronous operations concurrently.

Example of Parallel Processing:

```csharp
Copy code
public async Task ProcessImagesInParallelAsync(IEnumerable<string> imagePaths)
{
    var tasks = imagePaths.Select(async path =>
    {
        var image = await LoadImageAsync(path);
        var resizedImage = ResizeImage(image);
        await SaveImageToDatabaseAsync(resizedImage);
    });

    await Task.WhenAll(tasks);
}
```

In this example, the image processing tasks are executed in parallel, allowing the application to handle multiple images simultaneously, thereby improving performance.

8.4 Scenario 4: Real-Time Notifications with SignalR

Real-time applications benefit greatly from asynchronous programming. This section explores how to implement real-time notifications using SignalR in a C# web application.

8.4.1 Setting Up SignalR

SignalR is a library that simplifies adding real-time web functionality to applications. It allows bi-directional communication between clients and servers. To use SignalR, you must install the appropriate NuGet packages and configure the services in your ASP.NET Core application.

Example of SignalR Setup:

```csharp
Copy code
public void ConfigureServices(IServiceCollection services)
{
    services.AddSignalR();
}

public void Configure(IApplicationBuilder app, IWebHostEnvironment env)
{
    app.UseRouting();
    app.UseEndpoints(endpoints =>
    {
        endpoints.MapHub<NotificationHub>("/notifications");
    });
}
```

In this example, SignalR is configured in the Startup class, mapping the hub to a specific route.

8.4.2 Creating a Notification Hub

Create a SignalR hub that handles connections and sends notifications to clients.

Example of a Notification Hub:

```csharp
public class NotificationHub : Hub
{
    public async Task SendNotification(string message)
    {
        await Clients.All.SendAsync("ReceiveNotification",
        message);
    }
}
```

In this example, the SendNotification method broadcasts a message to all connected clients.

8.4.3 Client-Side Implementation

On the client side, use JavaScript to connect to the SignalR hub and handle incoming notifications.

Example of Client-Side SignalR Usage:

```javascript
const connection = new signalR.HubConnectionBuilder()
    .withUrl("/notifications")
    .build();

connection.on("ReceiveNotification", function (message) {
    console.log("New notification: " + message);
});

connection.start().catch(function (err) {
    return console.error(err.toString());
});
```

This JavaScript code connects to the SignalR hub and listens for notifications, ensuring that clients can receive real-time updates.

8.5 Scenario 5: Asynchronous Background Tasks with Hangfire

In many applications, background processing is essential for tasks such as sending emails, processing images, or performing scheduled jobs. This section explores how to implement asynchronous background tasks using **Hangfire** in C#.

8.5.1 Setting Up Hangfire

Hangfire is a library that allows you to perform background processing in .NET applications. To get started, install the Hangfire NuGet packages and configure it in your application.

Example of Hangfire Setup:

```csharp
Copy code
public void ConfigureServices(IServiceCollection services)
{
    services.AddHangfire(config =>
    config.UseSqlServerStorage("ConnectionString"));
    services.AddHangfireServer();
}

public void Configure(IApplicationBuilder app, IWebHostEnvironment env)
{
    app.UseHangfireDashboard();
    app.UseHangfireServer();
}
```

In this example, Hangfire is configured to use SQL Server for job storage, and the dashboard is set up for monitoring background jobs.

8.5.2 Defining Background Jobs

You can define background jobs using Hangfire, specifying whether they should run immediately, at a scheduled time, or recurrently.

Example of Defining a Background Job:

```csharp
Copy code
public void ScheduleEmailSending(string email)
{
```

```
    BackgroundJob.Enqueue(() => SendEmailAsync(email));
}

public async Task SendEmailAsync(string email)
{
    // Implementation for sending email
}
```

In this example, the ScheduleEmailSending method enqueues an email-sending job that will be processed in the background.

8.5.3 Monitoring Background Jobs

Hangfire provides a dashboard for monitoring the status of background jobs, allowing you to view their success, failure, and other statistics. Access the dashboard at /hangfire in your application.

Conclusion

In this chapter, we explored various real-world scenarios where asynchronous programming in C#12 can enhance application performance and responsiveness. We covered:

- Building a responsive web API using asynchronous techniques for data fetching and handling concurrency.
- Implementing asynchronous I/O operations in desktop applications to keep the UI responsive.
- Creating a data processing pipeline that leverages asynchronous programming to improve throughput.
- Using SignalR to implement real-time notifications in web applications.
- Implementing background tasks with Hangfire to offload long-running operations from the main application thread.

These case studies demonstrate how asynchronous programming can be applied in practical situations, allowing developers to create efficient, responsive applications. In the next chapter, we will delve into **best practices**

for optimizing asynchronous applications, covering advanced techniques for maximizing performance and efficiency.

Chapter 9: Best Practices for Optimizing Asynchronous Applications in C#12

Asynchronous programming in C#12 offers tremendous benefits for building responsive and scalable applications. However, writing asynchronous code is only the first step; optimizing that code for performance and reliability is crucial. In this chapter, we will explore best practices for optimizing asynchronous applications, including memory management, reducing latency, handling exceptions, and testing strategies.

9.1 Understanding Performance Optimization in Asynchronous Applications

Optimizing asynchronous applications involves a combination of strategies that enhance responsiveness, reduce memory usage, and improve overall efficiency. This section outlines the key areas to focus on for effective optimization.

9.1.1 Identifying Performance Bottlenecks

Before optimizing your asynchronous application, it's essential to identify performance bottlenecks. Common areas to investigate include:

- **Long-running Tasks**: Identify tasks that take an excessive amount of time to complete, which may block other operations.
- **Excessive Memory Usage**: Monitor memory allocation patterns to detect memory leaks or unnecessary allocations.

- **Inefficient I/O Operations**: Analyze the performance of I/O-bound operations to ensure they are optimized for speed and responsiveness.

9.1.2 Setting Performance Goals

Establish clear performance goals for your application, such as response time, throughput, and resource utilization. These goals will guide your optimization efforts and help you measure success.

Example Performance Goals:

- Maintain a response time of less than 200 milliseconds for API requests.
- Support at least 100 concurrent users without degradation in performance.
- Reduce memory usage by 30% compared to the previous version.

9.2 Memory Management in Asynchronous Applications

Efficient memory management is critical for optimizing asynchronous applications. This section covers techniques to minimize memory usage and prevent memory leaks.

9.2.1 Minimizing Object Allocations

Frequent object allocations can lead to increased garbage collection overhead and memory pressure. To minimize allocations:

- **Use Structs Instead of Classes**: For small data types that do not require inheritance or polymorphism, prefer structs to reduce heap allocations.

Example:

```csharp
Copy code
public struct Point
{
    public int X;
    public int Y;
```

CHAPTER 9: BEST PRACTICES FOR OPTIMIZING ASYNCHRONOUS...

}

- **Reuse Objects**: Implement object pooling for frequently used objects to reduce the need for allocations.

Example:

```csharp
Copy code
private static readonly ObjectPool<MyObject> _pool = new DefaultObjectPool<MyObject>(new DefaultPooledObjectPolicy<MyObject>());

public void SomeMethod()
{
    var obj = _pool.Get();
    try
    {
        // Use obj
    }
    finally
    {
        _pool.Return(obj);
    }
}
```

9.2.2 Avoiding Memory Leaks

Memory leaks occur when references to objects are not released, preventing them from being garbage collected. To avoid memory leaks:

- **Unsubscribe from Events**: Always unsubscribe from events when they are no longer needed, especially in long-lived objects.

Example:

```csharp
Copy code
public class MyClass
{
    public MyClass(EventPublisher publisher)
    {
        publisher.SomeEvent += OnSomeEvent;
    }

    private void OnSomeEvent(object sender, EventArgs e)
    {
        // Handle event
    }

    public void Dispose()
    {
        publisher.SomeEvent -= OnSomeEvent; // Unsubscribe
    }
}
```

- **Weak References**: Use WeakReference when holding references to large objects or event handlers that should not prevent garbage collection.

9.2.3 Monitoring Memory Usage

Utilize profiling tools to monitor memory usage and identify potential leaks. Tools like Visual Studio's Diagnostic Tools and JetBrains dotMemory provide insights into memory allocation patterns and help diagnose issues.

Example of Running a Memory Profiler:

1. Open your project in Visual Studio.
2. Start debugging your application.
3. Use the Diagnostic Tools to monitor memory allocation.

By actively monitoring memory usage, you can address issues before they impact performance.

CHAPTER 9: BEST PRACTICES FOR OPTIMIZING ASYNCHRONOUS...

9.3 Reducing Latency in Asynchronous Applications

Reducing latency is crucial for maintaining responsiveness in asynchronous applications. This section covers strategies to minimize latency in various scenarios.

9.3.1 Avoiding Blocking Calls

Ensure that your asynchronous methods do not call synchronous blocking methods. Always use the asynchronous versions of I/O operations to maintain responsiveness.

Example:

```csharp
Copy code
public async Task<string> ReadFileAsync(string filePath)
{
    using var stream = new FileStream(filePath, FileMode.Open,
    FileAccess.Read, FileShare.Read, 4096, true);
    using var reader = new StreamReader(stream);
    return await reader.ReadToEndAsync();
}
```

By avoiding blocking calls, you allow the application to continue processing other tasks.

9.3.2 Optimizing I/O Operations

I/O-bound tasks often introduce latency. To optimize I/O operations:

- **Batch I/O Requests**: Combine multiple I/O requests into a single operation to reduce round trips.

Example:

```csharp
Copy code
public async Task<List<string>>
ReadMultipleFilesAsync(IEnumerable<string> filePaths)
{
```

```
    var tasks = filePaths.Select(filePath =>
    ReadFileAsync(filePath));
    return await Task.WhenAll(tasks);
}
```

- **Use Buffered I/O**: Implement buffered I/O operations to read and write data in chunks, minimizing the number of I/O operations.

9.3.3 Asynchronous Caching

Implement caching strategies to reduce latency for frequently accessed data. Caching can significantly improve performance by minimizing the need for repeated I/O operations.

Example:

```csharp
Copy code
private static readonly MemoryCache _cache = new MemoryCache(new MemoryCacheOptions());

public async Task<string> GetDataWithCacheAsync(string key)
{
    if (!_cache.TryGetValue(key, out string cachedData))
    {
        cachedData = await FetchDataFromSourceAsync(key);
        _cache.Set(key, cachedData, TimeSpan.FromMinutes(5));
    }
    return cachedData;
}
```

In this example, data is cached for five minutes, reducing latency for subsequent requests.

9.4 Exception Handling Strategies in Asynchronous Applications

Effective exception handling is crucial for maintaining the stability of asynchronous applications. This section discusses strategies for handling exceptions in asynchronous code.

9.4.1 Global Exception Handling

Implement global exception handling mechanisms to capture unhandled exceptions in your application. This can be done using middleware in ASP.NET Core applications.

Example of Global Exception Handling Middleware:

```csharp
Copy code
public class ExceptionHandlingMiddleware
{
    private readonly RequestDelegate _next;

    public ExceptionHandlingMiddleware(RequestDelegate next)
    {
        _next = next;
    }

    public async Task InvokeAsync(HttpContext context)
    {
        try
        {
            await _next(context);
        }
        catch (Exception ex)
        {
            // Log the exception
            await HandleExceptionAsync(context, ex);
        }
    }

    private Task HandleExceptionAsync(HttpContext context, Exception ex)
    {
        context.Response.ContentType = "application/json";
        context.Response.StatusCode = (int)HttpStatusCode.InternalServerError;
        return context.Response.WriteAsync(new { error = ex.Message }.ToString());
    }
```

}

By implementing global exception handling, you can ensure that unhandled exceptions are logged and that the application responds gracefully.

9.4.2 Graceful Degradation

Design your application to degrade gracefully in the event of failures. For instance, if a service call fails, provide fallback mechanisms or default values to maintain application functionality.

Example of Fallback Logic:

```csharp
Copy code
public async Task<string> GetDataWithFallbackAsync(string url)
{
    try
    {
        return await httpClient.GetStringAsync(url);
    }
    catch (HttpRequestException)
    {
        return "Default Data"; // Fallback value
    }
}
```

By implementing fallback logic, you can ensure that your application continues to function, even in the face of errors.

9.5 Testing Strategies for Asynchronous Applications

Testing asynchronous applications requires different approaches than traditional synchronous testing. This section covers best practices for testing asynchronous code effectively.

9.5.1 Unit Testing Asynchronous Methods

When writing unit tests for asynchronous methods, ensure that your testing framework supports asynchronous test methods. Most modern frameworks, like xUnit and NUnit, allow you to define asynchronous tests using the async keyword.

Example of an Asynchronous Unit Test:

```csharp
Copy code
[Fact]
public async Task FetchDataAsync_ReturnsExpectedData()
{
    var service = new DataService();
    var expectedData = "Hello, World!";

    var result = await service.FetchDataAsync();

    Assert.Equal(expectedData, result);
}
```

In this example, the asynchronous test method is defined using async, allowing for proper awaiting of the asynchronous operation.

9.5.2 Mocking Asynchronous Dependencies

When testing asynchronous methods that rely on external dependencies, use mocking frameworks to simulate the behavior of those dependencies. This helps isolate the method under test.

Example of Mocking with Moq:

```csharp
Copy code
var mockHttpClient = new Mock<IHttpClient>();
mockHttpClient.Setup(client =>
client.GetStringAsync(It.IsAny<string>()))
            .ReturnsAsync("Mocked Data");

var service = new DataService(mockHttpClient.Object);
var result = await service.FetchDataAsync();

Assert.Equal("Mocked Data", result);
```

By mocking dependencies, you ensure that your tests are fast and reliable, focusing solely on the behavior of the method being tested.

9.5.3 Integration Testing for Asynchronous Workflows

Integration testing is essential for validating the behavior of asynchronous methods in the context of the entire application. Ensure that your integration tests use real dependencies to verify end-to-end functionality.

Example of an Integration Test:

```csharp
Copy code
[Fact]
public async Task ProcessDataAsync_SavesDataCorrectly()
{
    var service = new DataService();
    await service.ProcessDataAsync();

    var data = await service.GetSavedDataAsync();
    Assert.NotNull(data);
    Assert.Equal("Expected Value", data.Value);
}
```

In this example, the integration test verifies that the ProcessDataAsync method correctly saves data using real dependencies.

9.6 Continuous Monitoring and Performance Tuning

After deploying an asynchronous application, continuous monitoring is essential to ensure that it performs as expected under real-world conditions. This section covers strategies for ongoing performance tuning.

9.6.1 Using Application Performance Monitoring (APM) Tools

APM tools like **Application Insights** and **New Relic** provide real-time monitoring of application performance, allowing you to track response times, error rates, and resource utilization.

Example of Setting Up Application Insights:

1. Install the Application Insights SDK via NuGet.
2. Configure Application Insights in your application's Startup class.

CHAPTER 9: BEST PRACTICES FOR OPTIMIZING ASYNCHRONOUS...

```csharp
Copy code
public void ConfigureServices(IServiceCollection services)
{
    services.AddApplicationInsightsTelemetry();
}
```

1. Monitor application performance and identify bottlenecks using the Azure portal.

Using APM tools helps you gain insights into the behavior of your asynchronous applications, enabling proactive performance tuning.

9.6.2 Performance Profiling

Conduct regular performance profiling to identify slow-running tasks, excessive memory allocations, and other performance issues. Profiling tools like Visual Studio's Performance Profiler or JetBrains dotTrace can help you gather insights.

Example of Running a Performance Profiler:

1. Open your project in Visual Studio.
2. Start debugging and select **Performance Profiler** from the **Debug** menu.
3. Choose the profiling options (e.g., CPU Usage, Memory Usage) and analyze the results.

By profiling your application, you can pinpoint performance issues and make informed optimization decisions.

Conclusion

In this chapter, we explored best practices for optimizing asynchronous applications in C#12. We covered various critical aspects, including:

- Understanding performance optimization and identifying bottlenecks.
- Techniques for efficient memory management to minimize usage and prevent leaks.
- Strategies to reduce latency in asynchronous operations.
- Exception handling strategies to ensure robust error management.
- Testing strategies for effectively validating asynchronous code, including unit and integration testing.
- Continuous monitoring and performance tuning to maintain optimal application performance.

By following these best practices, you can create high-performance, responsive asynchronous applications that meet the demands of modern software development. In the next chapter, we will delve into advanced topics, including advanced asynchronous programming patterns and their applications in C#12.

Chapter 10: Advanced Topics in Asynchronous Programming with C#12

Asynchronous programming is a powerful paradigm that allows developers to build responsive and scalable applications. In this chapter, we will delve into advanced topics in asynchronous programming with C#12, exploring sophisticated patterns and techniques that can enhance your application's performance and maintainability. We will cover reactive programming, task-based workflows, integration with other paradigms, and real-world implementations of these concepts.

10.1 Advanced Asynchronous Patterns

This section introduces advanced asynchronous programming patterns that can help solve complex problems and improve code organization.

10.1.1 Task-Based Asynchronous Pattern (TAP)

The Task-Based Asynchronous Pattern (TAP) is a fundamental asynchronous programming model in .NET. TAP provides a consistent approach to handling asynchronous operations using the Task class. Understanding TAP is essential for writing advanced asynchronous code.

Creating Tasks

Tasks can be created using the Task.Run method, which allows you to offload work to a separate thread. This is useful for CPU-bound operations that need to run in the background.

Example:

```csharp
Copy code
public async Task<int> CalculateSumAsync(int[] numbers)
{
    return await Task.Run(() =>
    {
        return numbers.Sum();
    });
}
```

In this example, the CalculateSumAsync method offloads the summation of an array to a separate thread, preventing blocking of the calling thread.

Handling Completion

Tasks can be combined using Task.WhenAll or Task.WhenAny. This allows you to manage multiple asynchronous operations efficiently.

Example of Task.WhenAll:

```csharp
Copy code
public async Task ProcessMultipleTasksAsync(IEnumerable<Task> tasks)
{
    await Task.WhenAll(tasks);
}
```

This example waits for all tasks to complete, allowing you to perform actions once all operations are finished.

10.1.2 Reactive Programming

Reactive programming is a paradigm that focuses on building asynchronous, event-driven systems. It allows developers to work with data streams and react to changes in real time. In C#12, the Reactive Extensions (Rx) library provides powerful tools for implementing reactive programming.

Creating Observables

Observables are the core concept in reactive programming, allowing you

CHAPTER 10: ADVANCED TOPICS IN ASYNCHRONOUS PROGRAMMING WITH...

to represent asynchronous data streams. You can create an observable using Observable.Create.

Example:

```csharp
Copy code
var observable = Observable.Create<string>(observer =>
{
    observer.OnNext("Hello");
    observer.OnNext("World");
    observer.OnCompleted();
    return Disposable.Empty;
});
```

In this example, an observable emits a series of strings. Consumers can subscribe to this observable to receive updates.

Subscribing to Observables

Consumers can subscribe to observables to receive data and handle events.

Example:

```csharp
Copy code
observable.Subscribe(
    data => Console.WriteLine($"Received: {data}"),
    ex => Console.WriteLine($"Error: {ex.Message}"),
    () => Console.WriteLine("Completed")
);
```

This code subscribes to the observable, logging each emitted value and handling errors and completion notifications.

10.1.3 Combining Async and Reactive Programming

You can combine asynchronous programming with reactive programming to handle complex workflows and manage data streams efficiently. This allows you to build responsive applications that react to events and changes in real time.

Using Async with Rx

Rx supports asynchronous operations natively. You can convert asynchronous methods to observables using Observable.FromAsync.

Example:

```csharp
Copy code
public IObservable<string> GetDataObservable()
{
    return Observable.FromAsync(async () =>
    {
        using var client = new HttpClient();
        return await
        client.GetStringAsync("https://api.example.com/data");
    });
}
```

In this example, the GetDataObservable method converts an asynchronous HTTP request into an observable, allowing consumers to subscribe to it.

10.2 Task-Based Workflows

Task-based workflows allow you to model complex operations that involve multiple asynchronous tasks. This section explores how to design and implement task-based workflows effectively.

10.2.1 Chaining Tasks

Chaining tasks is a common pattern in asynchronous programming. You can create a workflow by chaining multiple tasks using ContinueWith or await.

Example of Chaining with Await:

```csharp
Copy code
public async Task<string> FetchAndProcessDataAsync(string url)
{
    var data = await FetchDataAsync(url);
    return ProcessData(data);
}
```

CHAPTER 10: ADVANCED TOPICS IN ASYNCHRONOUS PROGRAMMING WITH...

In this example, the FetchAndProcessDataAsync method fetches data asynchronously and processes it in a single workflow.

10.2.2 Handling Task Results

When chaining tasks, you may need to handle results from multiple tasks. Use tuple or custom data structures to manage and return results effectively.

Example of Returning Multiple Results:

```csharp
Copy code
public async Task<(string data, int statusCode)> FetchDataWithStatusAsync(string url)
{
    var response = await httpClient.GetAsync(url);
    var data = await response.Content.ReadAsStringAsync();
    return (data, (int)response.StatusCode);
}
```

This method returns a tuple containing both the fetched data and the HTTP status code, making it easy to work with multiple results.

10.2.3 Implementing Complex Workflows with Async/Await

You can model complex workflows using async/await for better readability and maintainability. Break down the workflow into smaller, reusable methods.

Example of a Complex Workflow:

```csharp
Copy code
public async Task ProcessOrderAsync(Order order)
{
    var product = await FetchProductAsync(order.ProductId);
    var customer = await FetchCustomerAsync(order.CustomerId);
    await ChargeCustomerAsync(customer, product.Price);
    await NotifyCustomerAsync(customer);
}
```

In this example, the ProcessOrderAsync method handles a series of asynchronous operations, making the workflow easy to follow.

10.3 Integrating Asynchronous Programming with Other Paradigms

Asynchronous programming can be integrated with other programming paradigms, such as functional programming and microservices. This section explores how to leverage these paradigms in conjunction with asynchronous programming.

10.3.1 Functional Programming with Async

Functional programming emphasizes immutability and pure functions, which can enhance the design of asynchronous applications. When designing asynchronous APIs, consider using higher-order functions that accept asynchronous callbacks or return asynchronous results.

Example of Higher-Order Function:

```csharp
Copy code
public async Task<TResult>
ExecuteWithLoggingAsync<TResult>(Func<Task<TResult>> func)
{
    Console.WriteLine("Execution started.");
    var result = await func();
    Console.WriteLine("Execution finished.");
    return result;
}
```

This higher-order function logs the execution of any asynchronous operation passed to it.

10.3.2 Microservices Architecture

In microservices architecture, asynchronous communication patterns are crucial for building scalable and resilient systems. Use message queues (e.g., RabbitMQ, Azure Service Bus) to enable asynchronous communication between services.

Example of Sending a Message to a Queue:

```csharp
Copy code
```

CHAPTER 10: ADVANCED TOPICS IN ASYNCHRONOUS PROGRAMMING WITH...

```csharp
public async Task SendMessageAsync(Message message)
{
    var queueClient = new QueueClient(connectionString,
        queueName);
    await queueClient.SendAsync(message);
}
```

In this example, the SendMessageAsync method sends a message to a queue asynchronously, allowing the application to decouple services and enhance scalability.

10.3.3 Asynchronous Streams in Functional Pipelines

Asynchronous streams can be combined with functional programming techniques to create data processing pipelines. Use LINQ-like operations to transform and filter data in a non-blocking manner.

Example of Asynchronous Stream Processing:

```csharp
Copy code
public async IAsyncEnumerable<string>
    ProcessDataAsync(IEnumerable<string> data)
{
    foreach (var item in data)
    {
        var processedItem = await ProcessItemAsync(item);
        yield return processedItem;
    }
}
```

In this example, ProcessDataAsync processes each item in an asynchronous stream, allowing consumers to iterate over the results incrementally.

10.4 Real-World Implementation: Building an Asynchronous Chat Application

In this section, we will demonstrate how to build a simple asynchronous chat application using C#12, incorporating many of the techniques discussed in this chapter.

10.4.1 Setting Up the Project

Create a new ASP.NET Core Web Application project and set up SignalR for real-time communication. Install the necessary NuGet packages for SignalR.

```bash
Copy code
dotnet new webapp -n ChatApp
cd ChatApp
dotnet add package Microsoft.AspNetCore.SignalR
```

10.4.2 Designing the Chat Hub

Create a SignalR hub to manage connections and facilitate message exchanges between clients.

Example of a Chat Hub:

```csharp
Copy code
public class ChatHub : Hub
{
    public async Task SendMessage(string user, string message)
    {
        await Clients.All.SendAsync("ReceiveMessage", user,
            message);
    }
}
```

In this example, the SendMessage method sends messages to all connected clients.

10.4.3 Implementing the Client-Side Logic

Create a simple HTML page with JavaScript to handle user interactions and display messages. Use SignalR's JavaScript client to connect to the chat hub.

Example of Client-Side JavaScript:

CHAPTER 10: ADVANCED TOPICS IN ASYNCHRONOUS PROGRAMMING WITH...

```html
Copy code
<script src="https://cdnjs.cloudflare.com/ajax/libs/microsoft.signalr/5.0.0/signalr.min.js"></script>
<script>
    const connection = new signalR.HubConnectionBuilder()
        .withUrl("/chatHub")
        .build();

    connection.on("ReceiveMessage", (user, message) => {
        const msg = document.createElement("div");
        msg.textContent = `${user}: ${message}`;
        document.getElementById("messagesList").appendChild(msg);
    });

    connection.start().catch(err => console.error(err));

    document.getElementById("sendButton").addEventListener("click", async () => {
        const user = document.getElementById("userInput").value;
        const message = document.getElementById("messageInput").value;
        await connection.invoke("SendMessage", user, message);
        document.getElementById("messageInput").value = "";
    });
</script>
```

In this JavaScript code, we handle incoming messages and allow users to send messages via the chat hub.

10.4.4 Testing the Chat Application

Once the chat application is set up, test it by running multiple instances of the client (e.g., opening multiple browser tabs) and sending messages. Ensure that all clients receive the messages in real-time, demonstrating the power of asynchronous programming and SignalR.

10.5 Advanced Debugging Techniques for Asynchronous Code

Debugging asynchronous code can be challenging due to its non-blocking nature. This section discusses advanced debugging techniques to help troubleshoot asynchronous applications effectively.

10.5.1 Using Visual Studio Debugger

Visual Studio provides robust debugging tools that allow you to inspect asynchronous code execution. Use breakpoints, watch windows, and the Call Stack to analyze the flow of asynchronous methods.

Example of Setting Breakpoints:

- Set breakpoints on asynchronous methods to observe their execution.
- Use the Call Stack window to track the order of method calls, including continuations.

10.5.2 Debugging Tasks in Visual Studio

When debugging tasks, you can use the Tasks window to monitor the status of running tasks. This allows you to see which tasks are running, completed, or faulted.

Steps to Monitor Tasks:

1. Start debugging your application.
2. Open the **Tasks** window from the Debug menu.
3. Observe the status of tasks in real-time.

By leveraging Visual Studio's debugging features, you can gain valuable insights into the behavior of asynchronous code.

Conclusion

In this chapter, we explored advanced topics in asynchronous programming with C#12, focusing on sophisticated patterns and techniques that enhance application performance and maintainability. Key areas covered include:

- Advanced asynchronous patterns, including Task-Based Asynchronous

Pattern (TAP) and reactive programming.
- Designing task-based workflows to manage complex asynchronous operations.
- Integrating asynchronous programming with functional programming and microservices architecture.
- Real-world implementation of an asynchronous chat application using SignalR.
- Advanced debugging techniques to troubleshoot asynchronous code effectively.

By mastering these advanced topics, you can harness the full power of asynchronous programming in C#12, enabling you to build high-performance, responsive applications that meet the demands of modern software development. In the next chapter, we will summarize the key concepts covered throughout the book and discuss future directions for asynchronous programming in C#.

Chapter 11: Future Directions in Asynchronous Programming with C#12

Asynchronous programming has transformed how developers approach application design and performance, especially with the advancements in C#12 and the .NET ecosystem. This chapter examines the future directions of asynchronous programming, highlighting emerging trends, evolving technologies, and best practices that developers should adopt to stay relevant in this rapidly changing landscape.

11.1 The Evolution of Asynchronous Programming

Asynchronous programming has evolved significantly over the years. From the early days of callback-based programming to the introduction of the Task-Based Asynchronous Pattern (TAP), the evolution of C# and .NET has enabled developers to write cleaner, more manageable asynchronous code.

11.1.1 Early Models of Asynchronous Programming

Before C# adopted TAP, asynchronous programming was primarily managed through callback methods, which often led to "callback hell" — a situation where multiple nested callbacks made the code difficult to read and maintain.

Example of Callback Hell:

```csharp
Copy code
FetchData(url, (data) => {
    ProcessData(data, (processed) => {
        SaveData(processed, (result) => {
            // Handle result
        });
    });
});
```

This style of programming was not only challenging to read but also difficult to debug, leading to the need for better models.

11.1.2 The Introduction of TAP

With the introduction of TAP in C# 5.0, developers gained a structured way to write asynchronous code. TAP allows developers to use async and await keywords to write asynchronous operations that look synchronous, improving readability and maintainability.

Example of TAP:

```csharp
Copy code
public async Task<string> FetchDataAsync(string url)
{
    using var client = new HttpClient();
    return await client.GetStringAsync(url);
}
```

This shift from callbacks to TAP has laid the groundwork for more sophisticated asynchronous patterns that are now emerging in the C# ecosystem.

11.2 Emerging Trends in Asynchronous Programming

As technology advances, new trends and practices in asynchronous programming are becoming prevalent. Understanding these trends can help developers prepare for the future of software development.

11.2.1 The Rise of Asynchronous Streams

Asynchronous streams, introduced in C# 8.0, have gained popularity for handling data that arrives over time. This paradigm allows developers to process data incrementally, improving performance and responsiveness.

Example of Asynchronous Streams:

```csharp
Copy code
public async IAsyncEnumerable<int> GenerateNumbersAsync()
{
    for (int i = 0; i < 100; i++)
    {
        await Task.Delay(100); // Simulate delay
        yield return i; // Yield numbers asynchronously
    }
}
```

Asynchronous streams are particularly useful in scenarios involving real-time data processing, such as handling live data feeds or streaming APIs.

11.2.2 The Integration of Reactive Programming

Reactive programming continues to gain traction as developers seek ways to build responsive applications that react to changes in data and events. Libraries like Reactive Extensions (Rx) allow developers to compose asynchronous and event-based programs using observable sequences.

Example of Reactive Programming with Rx:

```csharp
Copy code
var observable = Observable.Interval(TimeSpan.FromSeconds(1));
observable.Subscribe(x => Console.WriteLine($"Tick: {x}"));
```

As applications become more complex, integrating reactive programming with asynchronous patterns will provide powerful tools for handling asynchronous data flows.

11.2.3 Improved Debugging and Diagnostic Tools

As asynchronous programming becomes more prevalent, the need for advanced debugging and diagnostic tools is paramount. Future versions

CHAPTER 11: FUTURE DIRECTIONS IN ASYNCHRONOUS PROGRAMMING...

of Visual Studio and .NET are likely to include enhanced profiling tools specifically designed for asynchronous code.

These tools may offer features such as:

- **Visualizing Task Execution**: Graphical representations of task execution timelines to help developers understand how tasks are running in parallel.
- **Automatic Detection of Deadlocks**: Enhanced analysis tools that automatically detect potential deadlocks in asynchronous workflows.
- **Memory Profiling for Async**: Advanced memory profiling tools to track memory allocations specific to asynchronous operations.

11.3 Best Practices for Future-Proofing Asynchronous Code

As the landscape of asynchronous programming evolves, adopting best practices will help developers create robust and maintainable code that stands the test of time.

11.3.1 Embrace Asynchronous by Default

When designing APIs or components, consider making asynchronous methods the default. This approach encourages best practices and aligns with modern application architecture.

Example:

```csharp
Copy code
public async Task<string> GetDataAsync(); // Default async
public string GetData(); // Optional sync
```

By providing asynchronous versions as the primary methods, you enable consumers to adopt asynchronous programming easily.

11.3.2 Prioritize Readability and Maintainability

Asynchronous code should be as readable and maintainable as synchronous code. Use meaningful method names, consistent naming conventions, and well-structured error handling to enhance code quality.

Example of Readable Async Code:

```csharp
Copy code
public async Task<string> FetchUserDataAsync(int userId)
{
    try
    {
        return await database.GetUserDataAsync(userId);
    }
    catch (Exception ex)
    {
        // Handle exception gracefully
        throw new DataFetchException("Unable to fetch user
        data.", ex);
    }
}
```

Prioritizing readability makes it easier for other developers to understand and work with your code.

11.3.3 Educate Teams on Asynchronous Patterns

Invest in training and education for your development team to ensure that everyone is on the same page regarding asynchronous programming practices. This can involve:

- **Workshops**: Organize workshops to explore asynchronous programming concepts and best practices.
- **Documentation**: Provide comprehensive documentation and coding standards related to asynchronous programming.
- **Code Reviews**: Encourage code reviews focusing on asynchronous patterns to promote learning and adherence to best practices.

By fostering a culture of learning, you can enhance your team's ability to write high-quality asynchronous code.

11.4 Looking Ahead: C# and .NET Enhancements

The future of asynchronous programming in C#12 and .NET will likely include new features and enhancements that make it easier to work with asynchronous code.

11.4.1 Potential Language Features

Future versions of C# may introduce new language features aimed at improving the asynchronous programming experience. Some potential enhancements could include:

- **Improved Syntax for Async Streams**: Enhanced syntax for working with asynchronous streams, making it easier to compose and manipulate data flows.
- **More Powerful Task Combinators**: New combinators for tasks that allow for more expressive asynchronous workflows, potentially inspired by functional programming concepts.

11.4.2 Enhancements in the .NET Ecosystem

The .NET ecosystem will continue to evolve, with improvements to libraries and frameworks that support asynchronous programming. Key areas of focus may include:

- **Performance Improvements**: Ongoing efforts to optimize the performance of asynchronous I/O operations and memory management in the .NET runtime.
- **Better Integration with Cloud Services**: Enhanced libraries for integrating with cloud services, enabling seamless asynchronous communication with serverless architectures and event-driven systems.

By staying informed about future enhancements, developers can leverage new features to improve their asynchronous applications.

11.5 Conclusion

In this chapter, we explored the future directions of asynchronous programming in C#12, covering emerging trends, best practices, and anticipated enhancements in the language and framework. Key takeaways include:

- The evolution of asynchronous programming from early callback patterns to the adoption of TAP and reactive programming.
- Emerging trends such as asynchronous streams and the integration of reactive programming techniques.
- Best practices for future-proofing asynchronous code, including embracing async by default, prioritizing readability, and educating teams.
- Anticipated language features and enhancements in the .NET ecosystem that will continue to improve the asynchronous programming experience.

By understanding these trends and best practices, developers can position themselves to take full advantage of asynchronous programming in C#12, building responsive, efficient, and maintainable applications that meet the demands of modern software development.

In the concluding chapter, we will summarize the key concepts covered throughout the book and reflect on the importance of asynchronous programming in today's development landscape.

Chapter 12: Conclusion and Key Takeaways from Asynchronous Programming with C#12

Asynchronous programming is no longer just a niche concept reserved for specific scenarios; it has become an essential aspect of modern software development. With the introduction of C#12 and the continuous evolution of the .NET ecosystem, developers have powerful tools at their disposal to create responsive, efficient, and scalable applications. This concluding chapter summarizes the key concepts discussed throughout this book, highlights the importance of asynchronous programming, and offers final thoughts for developers aiming to enhance their skills in this area.

12.1 Recap of Key Concepts

Throughout this book, we explored a wide range of topics related to asynchronous programming in C#12. Here are the key concepts covered:

12.1.1 Understanding Asynchronous Programming

We began by establishing the foundation of asynchronous programming, distinguishing it from synchronous programming. The benefits of asynchronous programming include improved responsiveness, efficient resource utilization, and the ability to perform multiple operations concurrently.

12.1.2 The Task-Based Asynchronous Pattern (TAP)

The introduction of TAP revolutionized the way developers write asynchronous code in C#. The use of async and await keywords simplifies the syntax and improves readability, allowing developers to write asynchronous methods that resemble synchronous code.

Key Example:

```csharp
Copy code
public async Task<string> FetchDataAsync(string url)
{
    using var client = new HttpClient();
    return await client.GetStringAsync(url);
}
```

12.1.3 Error Handling and Best Practices

We emphasized the importance of robust error handling in asynchronous applications. Properly propagating exceptions, implementing global exception handling, and providing meaningful error messages were discussed as essential practices for maintaining application stability.

Key Example:

```csharp
Copy code
try
{
    var data = await FetchDataAsync(url);
}
catch (HttpRequestException ex)
{
    // Handle the exception
}
```

12.1.4 Testing Asynchronous Code

Testing asynchronous methods requires a different approach than traditional synchronous testing. We explored best practices for unit testing asynchronous methods, including the use of mocking frameworks and

CHAPTER 12: CONCLUSION AND KEY TAKEAWAYS FROM ASYNCHRONOUS...

integration testing strategies.

Key Example:

```csharp
Copy code
var mockHttpClient = new Mock<IHttpClient>();
mockHttpClient.Setup(client =>
client.GetStringAsync(It.IsAny<string>()))
              .ReturnsAsync("Mocked Data");
```

12.1.5 Advanced Topics in Asynchronous Programming

The book also delved into advanced topics, including reactive programming, asynchronous streams, and task-based workflows. We explored how these advanced patterns can help developers build more responsive and maintainable applications.

Key Example:

```csharp
Copy code
public async IAsyncEnumerable<string> GenerateNumbersAsync()
{
    for (int i = 0; i < 100; i++)
    {
        await Task.Delay(100); // Simulate asynchronous work
        yield return i.ToString();
    }
}
```

12.1.6 Future Directions in Asynchronous Programming

Finally, we discussed the future of asynchronous programming, focusing on emerging trends and technologies. Topics included the rise of asynchronous streams, improved debugging tools, and the integration of asynchronous programming with other paradigms like reactive programming and microservices.

12.2 The Significance of Asynchronous Programming

Asynchronous programming has transformed the way developers approach application design and performance. The significance of asynchronous programming can be summarized as follows:

12.2.1 Enhanced Responsiveness

In today's applications, responsiveness is crucial. Users expect applications to be fast and responsive, even when performing time-consuming operations. Asynchronous programming allows developers to keep the UI responsive by offloading long-running tasks to background threads.

12.2.2 Efficient Resource Utilization

Asynchronous programming enables more efficient use of system resources. By freeing up threads while waiting for I/O operations to complete, applications can handle more concurrent users and operations without requiring additional hardware resources.

12.2.3 Scalability

Asynchronous programming supports scalable architectures, particularly in web applications and microservices. By utilizing asynchronous I/O and non-blocking patterns, applications can scale to handle high loads without degrading performance.

12.2.4 Improved User Experience

Ultimately, the goal of asynchronous programming is to enhance the user experience. By providing fast, responsive applications that can handle real-time updates and background processing, developers can create applications that users love and find easy to use.

12.3 Final Thoughts and Recommendations

Asynchronous programming is a vital skill for modern developers. Here are some final thoughts and recommendations for developers looking to deepen their understanding and expertise in this area:

12.3.1 Practice Regularly

The best way to master asynchronous programming is through practice. Build small projects that utilize asynchronous patterns, experiment with different techniques, and explore the capabilities of C#12. Regular practice will reinforce your understanding and help you become more comfortable with asynchronous programming.

12.3.2 Stay Informed

The technology landscape is continually evolving. Stay informed about new features, libraries, and best practices related to asynchronous programming. Follow industry blogs, participate in online communities, and attend conferences to learn from experts and share your experiences.

12.3.3 Collaborate with Others

Engage with other developers to share knowledge and experiences related to asynchronous programming. Collaborating on projects, participating in code reviews, and discussing challenges can provide valuable insights and help you improve your skills.

12.3.4 Focus on Code Quality

Prioritize writing clean, maintainable asynchronous code. Follow best practices for naming conventions, error handling, and documentation. Write unit tests for your asynchronous methods to ensure correctness and maintainability. High-quality code not only benefits you as a developer but also improves collaboration with your team.

12.3.5 Embrace New Patterns and Technologies

Asynchronous programming is a rapidly evolving field. Be open to adopting new patterns, frameworks, and technologies that enhance your ability to build efficient and responsive applications. Experiment with reactive programming, asynchronous streams, and other emerging paradigms to expand your toolkit.

Conclusion

In conclusion, asynchronous programming with C#12 is a powerful paradigm that can significantly enhance the performance and responsiveness of applications. This book has provided a comprehensive overview of asynchronous programming concepts, best practices, and advanced topics. As you continue your journey in software development, embrace asynchronous programming to build applications that meet the demands of modern users and environments.

Asynchronous programming is not just a feature of C#12; it is a fundamental skill that every developer should master to stay competitive in today's fast-paced development landscape. By implementing the techniques and practices discussed in this book, you will be well-equipped to harness the full potential of asynchronous programming in your applications.

Chapter 13: Implementing Real-World Applications of Asynchronous Programming with C#12

Asynchronous programming has become a cornerstone of modern application development, enabling developers to create responsive, efficient, and scalable applications. In this chapter, we will explore various real-world applications of asynchronous programming in C#12, demonstrating how these techniques can be effectively implemented across different domains. By examining concrete examples and best practices, developers can gain insights into building robust asynchronous solutions that meet the demands of today's software landscape.

13.1 Building a Scalable Web API with Asynchronous Programming

In this section, we will discuss the implementation of a scalable web API that handles concurrent requests efficiently using asynchronous programming techniques.

13.1.1 Designing the API

When designing a web API, it is essential to consider the expected load and the types of operations that will be performed. For this example, we will create an online bookstore API that allows users to fetch book details, search for books, and place orders.

Defining the API Endpoints

We will define several endpoints for our API, including:
- GET /api/books: Retrieve a list of all books.
- GET /api/books/{id}: Retrieve details of a specific book.
- POST /api/orders: Place a new order.

13.1.2 Implementing Asynchronous Data Access

To implement asynchronous data access, we will use Entity Framework Core to interact with the database. We will create asynchronous methods for fetching and manipulating data.

Setting Up the Database Context

First, we need to set up the database context for our application:

```csharp
Copy code
public class BookstoreDbContext : DbContext
{
    public DbSet<Book> Books { get; set; }
    public DbSet<Order> Orders { get; set; }

    protected override void OnConfiguring(DbContextOptionsBuilder optionsBuilder)
    {
        optionsBuilder.UseSqlServer("YourConnectionString");
    }
}
```

Implementing Asynchronous Methods

Next, we will implement asynchronous methods in our service layer for data retrieval:

```csharp
Copy code
public class BookService
{
    private readonly BookstoreDbContext _context;
```

```csharp
public BookService(BookstoreDbContext context)
{
    _context = context;
}

public async Task<List<Book>> GetBooksAsync()
{
    return await _context.Books.ToListAsync();
}

public async Task<Book> GetBookByIdAsync(int id)
{
    return await _context.Books.FindAsync(id);
}

public async Task PlaceOrderAsync(Order order)
{
    _context.Orders.Add(order);
    await _context.SaveChangesAsync();
}
}
```

13.1.3 Creating the API Controller

With our service methods in place, we can now create an API controller to handle incoming requests.

Implementing the API Controller

```
csharp
Copy code
[ApiController]
[Route("api/[controller]")]
public class BooksController : ControllerBase
{
    private readonly BookService _bookService;

    public BooksController(BookService bookService)
    {
        _bookService = bookService;
```

```csharp
}

[HttpGet]
public async Task<ActionResult<List<Book>>> GetBooks()
{
    var books = await _bookService.GetBooksAsync();
    return Ok(books);
}

[HttpGet("{id}")]
public async Task<ActionResult<Book>> GetBook(int id)
{
    var book = await _bookService.GetBookByIdAsync(id);
    if (book == null)
    {
        return NotFound();
    }
    return Ok(book);
}

[HttpPost("orders")]
public async Task<ActionResult> PlaceOrder([FromBody] Order order)
{
    await _bookService.PlaceOrderAsync(order);
    return CreatedAtAction(nameof(GetBook), new { id = order.Id }, order);
}
}
```

In this implementation, the BooksController handles incoming HTTP requests asynchronously, ensuring that the API remains responsive even under load.

13.1.4 Handling Concurrency

In a web API, multiple clients may access or modify the same data simultaneously. Properly handling concurrency is essential for preventing data corruption.

Implementing Optimistic Concurrency Control

CHAPTER 13: IMPLEMENTING REAL-WORLD APPLICATIONS OF...

We can implement optimistic concurrency control using row versioning in Entity Framework Core. First, add a RowVersion property to the Book entity:

```csharp
public class Book
{
    public int Id { get; set; }
    public string Title { get; set; }
    public string Author { get; set; }
    [Timestamp]
    public byte[] RowVersion { get; set; }
}
```

Next, modify the PlaceOrderAsync method to handle concurrency exceptions:

```csharp
public async Task PlaceOrderAsync(Order order)
{
    try
    {
        _context.Orders.Add(order);
        await _context.SaveChangesAsync();
    }
    catch (DbUpdateConcurrencyException)
    {
        // Handle concurrency exception (e.g., notify the user)
        throw new Exception("The record you attempted to edit was modified by another user after you got the original value.");
    }
}
```

This approach allows the application to gracefully handle concurrency conflicts.

13.2 Creating a Responsive Desktop Application

This section will focus on building a responsive desktop application using asynchronous programming techniques, ensuring that the user interface remains responsive during long-running operations.

13.2.1 Designing the Application

For this example, we will create a simple Windows Forms application that allows users to download and display images from a URL. The application will fetch images asynchronously to prevent UI blocking.

13.2.2 Implementing Asynchronous Image Downloading

In our Windows Forms application, we will create a method to download images asynchronously:

Downloading Images Asynchronously

```csharp
Copy code
private async Task<Image> DownloadImageAsync(string url)
{
    using var client = new HttpClient();
    var imageBytes = await client.GetByteArrayAsync(url);
    using var ms = new MemoryStream(imageBytes);
    return Image.FromStream(ms);
}
```

13.2.3 Handling User Interaction

To ensure that the UI remains responsive, we will handle user interactions asynchronously. For instance, when a user clicks the "Download" button, we will initiate the download process.

Implementing the Download Button Click Event

```csharp
Copy code
private async void DownloadButton_Click(object sender, EventArgs e)
{
    string url = UrlTextBox.Text;
```

CHAPTER 13: IMPLEMENTING REAL-WORLD APPLICATIONS OF...

```csharp
    try
    {
        var image = await DownloadImageAsync(url);
        PictureBox.Image = image;
    }
    catch (Exception ex)
    {
        MessageBox.Show($"Error downloading image: {ex.Message}");
    }
}
```

In this implementation, the download operation runs asynchronously, allowing the UI to remain responsive while the image is being fetched.

13.2.4 Implementing Progress Reporting

To enhance the user experience, we can implement progress reporting to inform users about the download status.

Using IProgress<T> for Progress Reporting

```csharp
Copy code
private async Task<Image> DownloadImageAsync(string url,
IProgress<int> progress)
{
    using var client = new HttpClient();
    var response = await client.GetAsync(url,
HttpCompletionOption.ResponseHeadersRead);
    response.EnsureSuccessStatusCode();

    var totalBytes = response.Content.Headers.ContentLength ?? -1L;
    var imageBytes = new byte[totalBytes];
    var bytesRead = 0;

    using (var stream = await
response.Content.ReadAsStreamAsync())
    {
        while (bytesRead < totalBytes)
```

```
        {
            var read = await stream.ReadAsync(imageBytes,
            bytesRead, (int)(totalBytes - bytesRead));
            if (read == 0) break;

            bytesRead += read;
            progress.Report((int)((bytesRead * 100) /
            totalBytes));
        }
    }

    using var ms = new MemoryStream(imageBytes);
    return Image.FromStream(ms);
}
```

Updating the Progress Bar

In the button click event, we can update a progress bar based on the progress reported during the image download:

```csharp
Copy code
private async void DownloadButton_Click(object sender, EventArgs e)
{
    string url = UrlTextBox.Text;
    var progressIndicator = new Progress<int>(value =>
    ProgressBar.Value = value);

    try
    {
        var image = await DownloadImageAsync(url,
        progressIndicator);
        PictureBox.Image = image;
    }
    catch (Exception ex)
    {
        MessageBox.Show($"Error downloading image: {ex.Message}");
    }
```

}

This approach improves user experience by providing feedback on the download progress.

13.3 Implementing an Asynchronous Data Processing Pipeline

In this section, we will explore how to build an asynchronous data processing pipeline that processes large datasets efficiently.

13.3.1 Designing the Data Pipeline

We will create a data processing application that reads a large CSV file, processes each record asynchronously, and saves the results to a database. This design will allow for high throughput while minimizing memory usage.

13.3.2 Implementing Asynchronous File Reading

To read a CSV file asynchronously, we can use StreamReader to process each line incrementally:

```csharp
Copy code
public async IAsyncEnumerable<string> ReadLinesAsync(string filePath)
{
    using var reader = new StreamReader(filePath);
    while (!reader.EndOfStream)
    {
        var line = await reader.ReadLineAsync();
        yield return line;
    }
}
```

13.3.3 Processing Data Asynchronously

As we read each line, we can process the data asynchronously. In this example, we will simulate data processing by performing a simple transformation.

Processing Each Line

```csharp
Copy code
public async Task ProcessDataAsync(string filePath)
{
    await foreach (var line in ReadLinesAsync(filePath))
    {
        var processedData = await ProcessLineAsync(line);
        await SaveToDatabaseAsync(processedData);
    }
}

private async Task<string> ProcessLineAsync(string line)
{
    await Task.Delay(100); // Simulate processing time
    return line.ToUpper(); //
  Simple transformation for demonstration
}
```

In this example, each line is processed asynchronously, allowing the application to continue reading while processing takes place.

13.3.4 Saving Data to the Database

Finally, we will implement the method to save processed data to the database asynchronously:

```csharp
Copy code
public async Task SaveToDatabaseAsync(string data)
{
    using var context = new DataContext();
    var record = new DataRecord { Value = data };
    context.DataRecords.Add(record);
    await context.SaveChangesAsync();
}
```

This design allows for efficient data processing and saving, minimizing the time spent waiting for I/O operations.

13.4 Implementing Real-Time Features in a Chat Application

This section explores the implementation of real-time features in a chat application using asynchronous programming and SignalR.

13.4.1 Setting Up SignalR for Real-Time Communication

SignalR is a library that simplifies adding real-time web functionality to applications. To set up SignalR in an ASP.NET Core application, you need to install the necessary NuGet package and configure the services.

Installing SignalR

```bash
Copy code
dotnet add package Microsoft.AspNetCore.SignalR
```

Configuring SignalR in Startup

In the Startup.cs file, configure SignalR services:

```csharp
Copy code
public void ConfigureServices(IServiceCollection services)
{
    services.AddSignalR();
}

public void Configure(IApplicationBuilder app, IWebHostEnvironment env)
{
    app.UseRouting();
    app.UseEndpoints(endpoints =>
    {
        endpoints.MapHub<ChatHub>("/chatHub");
    });
}
```

13.4.2 Creating the Chat Hub

The chat hub will manage client connections and facilitate message exchanges. Here's how you can implement a simple chat hub:

```csharp
Copy code
public class ChatHub : Hub
{
    public async Task SendMessage(string user, string message)
    {
        await Clients.All.SendAsync("ReceiveMessage", user, message);
    }
}
```

In this example, the SendMessage method broadcasts messages to all connected clients.

13.4.3 Implementing the Client-Side Logic

On the client side, use JavaScript to connect to the SignalR hub and handle incoming messages.

Client-Side JavaScript Code

```html
Copy code
<script src="https://cdnjs.cloudflare.com/ajax/libs/microsoft.signalr/5.0.0/signalr.min.js"></script>
<script>
    const connection = new signalR.HubConnectionBuilder()
        .withUrl("/chatHub")
        .build();

    connection.on("ReceiveMessage", function (user, message) {
        const msg = document.createElement("div");
        msg.textContent = `${user}: ${message}`;
        document.getElementById("messagesList").appendChild(msg);
    });

    connection.start().catch(function (err) {
```

```
        return console.error(err.toString());
    });

    document.getElementById("sendButton").addEventListener("click",
    async () => {
        const user = document.getElementById("userInput").value;
        const message =
        document.getElementById("messageInput").value;
        await connection.invoke("SendMessage", user, message);
        document.getElementById("messageInput").value = "";
    });
</script>
```

This JavaScript code connects to the SignalR hub and listens for messages, displaying them in real-time as they arrive.

13.4.4 Testing the Chat Application

Once the chat application is set up, run multiple instances of the client (e.g., open several browser tabs) and send messages to test the real-time functionality. Each client should receive messages instantly, demonstrating the effectiveness of asynchronous programming and SignalR.

13.5 Conclusion

In this chapter, we explored various real-world applications of asynchronous programming in C#12. We covered:

- Building a scalable web API that efficiently handles concurrent requests using asynchronous programming techniques.
- Creating a responsive desktop application that downloads images asynchronously, ensuring a smooth user experience.
- Implementing an asynchronous data processing pipeline for reading and processing large datasets.
- Leveraging SignalR to add real-time features to a chat application, demonstrating the power of asynchronous programming for responsive interactions.

By examining these practical implementations, developers can gain valuable insights into applying asynchronous programming techniques effectively in their own applications. Embracing asynchronous programming enables the creation of modern, responsive, and scalable software that meets the expectations of users in today's fast-paced digital landscape.

Chapter 14: Best Practices for Maintaining Asynchronous Code in C#12

As applications grow in complexity and scale, maintaining high-quality asynchronous code becomes crucial for long-term success. This chapter discusses best practices for maintaining asynchronous code in C#12, emphasizing strategies for ensuring code quality, readability, performance, and collaboration within development teams. By adopting these practices, developers can create robust and maintainable asynchronous applications that stand the test of time.

14.1 Organizing Asynchronous Code for Clarity and Maintainability

A well-organized codebase is vital for maintaining asynchronous code. This section covers strategies for structuring your asynchronous code to enhance clarity and maintainability.

14.1.1 Use Meaningful Naming Conventions

Choosing meaningful names for your asynchronous methods is critical for readability. Follow consistent naming conventions to indicate the asynchronous nature of methods. For example, suffix method names with "Async" to denote that they perform asynchronous operations.

Example:

```csharp
Copy code
public async Task<List<Book>> FetchBooksAsync();
public async Task<bool> PlaceOrderAsync(Order order);
```

Using clear and descriptive names helps other developers understand the purpose and functionality of your methods at a glance.

14.1.2 Group Related Asynchronous Methods

Organize related asynchronous methods within the same class or service. Grouping methods by functionality enhances discoverability and promotes better encapsulation of related behaviors.

Example:

```csharp
Copy code
public class BookService
{
    public async Task<List<Book>> GetBooksAsync();
    public async Task<Book> GetBookByIdAsync(int id);
    public async Task PlaceOrderAsync(Order order);
}
```

This approach not only improves code organization but also makes it easier to maintain and update related methods.

14.1.3 Refactoring Long Asynchronous Methods

Long asynchronous methods can be challenging to read and understand. Refactor these methods into smaller, more manageable pieces, each focusing on a single responsibility.

Example:

```csharp
Copy code
```

CHAPTER 14: BEST PRACTICES FOR MAINTAINING ASYNCHRONOUS CODE...

```
public async Task ProcessOrderAsync(Order order)
{
    var book = await FetchBookAsync(order.BookId);
    var customer = await FetchCustomerAsync(order.CustomerId);
    await ChargeCustomerAsync(customer, book.Price);
    await NotifyCustomerAsync(customer);
}

// Refactored
public async Task ProcessOrderAsync(Order order)
{
    var book = await FetchBookAsync(order.BookId);
    await ProcessPaymentAsync(order.CustomerId, book.Price);
    await NotifyCustomerAsync(order.CustomerId);
}

private async Task ProcessPaymentAsync(int customerId, decimal amount)
{
    var customer = await FetchCustomerAsync(customerId);
    await ChargeCustomerAsync(customer, amount);
}
```

By breaking down the ProcessOrderAsync method, you improve readability and make future modifications easier.

14.2 Performance Monitoring and Optimization

Monitoring the performance of asynchronous code is critical for identifying bottlenecks and ensuring responsiveness. This section discusses strategies for effective performance monitoring and optimization.

14.2.1 Implementing Logging

Integrate logging into your asynchronous methods to track execution flow, monitor performance, and capture errors. Use structured logging to log relevant information, including method entry and exit, parameters, and execution time.

Example:

```csharp
Copy code
public async Task<string> FetchDataAsync(string url)
{
    var stopwatch = Stopwatch.StartNew();
    try
    {
        var data = await httpClient.GetStringAsync(url);
        return data;
    }
    catch (Exception ex)
    {
        logger.LogError(ex, "Error fetching data from {Url}",
        url);
        throw;
    }
    finally
    {
        stopwatch.Stop();
        logger.LogInformation("Fetched data from {Url} in
        {ElapsedMilliseconds} ms", url,
        stopwatch.ElapsedMilliseconds);
    }
}
```

In this example, logging provides insights into the execution of asynchronous methods and helps identify performance issues.

14.2.2 Profiling Asynchronous Code

Use profiling tools to analyze the performance of your asynchronous applications. Profilers can help identify slow-running tasks, excessive memory allocations, and bottlenecks in the execution flow.

Example of Using a Profiler:

- Utilize tools like **Visual Studio's Performance Profiler** or **dotTrace** to monitor CPU usage, memory allocations, and task execution times.
- Identify hot paths in your code and optimize them based on profiler feedback.

14.2.3 Analyzing Async Code Performance with Application Insights

Integrate Application Insights into your application to gain real-time insights into its performance. Application Insights provides monitoring for response times, failed requests, and usage patterns, allowing you to identify and address performance issues proactively.

Example:

```csharp
Copy code
public async Task<string> FetchDataAsync(string url)
{
    var telemetry = new TelemetryClient();
    var stopwatch = Stopwatch.StartNew();
    try
    {
        var data = await httpClient.GetStringAsync(url);
        return data;
    }
    finally
    {
        stopwatch.Stop();
        telemetry.TrackRequest("FetchData", DateTime.UtcNow,
        stopwatch.Elapsed, "200", true);
    }
}
```

By using Application Insights, you can monitor the health of your asynchronous operations in production.

14.3 Error Handling and Resilience

Effective error handling is essential for maintaining application stability. This section discusses best practices for managing errors in asynchronous applications.

14.3.1 Using Try-Catch Blocks

Wrap asynchronous calls in try-catch blocks to handle exceptions gracefully. This ensures that errors are captured, logged, and handled without crashing the application.

Example:

```csharp
Copy code
public async Task<string> FetchDataAsync(string url)
{
    try
    {
        return await httpClient.GetStringAsync(url);
    }
    catch (HttpRequestException ex)
    {
        logger.LogError(ex, "Failed to fetch data from {Url}", url);
        throw new DataFetchException("Error fetching data.", ex);
    }
}
```

In this example, exceptions are logged, and a custom exception is thrown to provide meaningful context.

14.3.2 Implementing Retry Logic

In scenarios where transient errors may occur (e.g., network issues), implementing retry logic can improve resilience. Use libraries like **Polly** to handle retries and circuit breakers for asynchronous calls.

Example of Using Polly for Retry Logic:

```csharp
Copy code
public async Task<string> FetchDataWithRetryAsync(string url)
{
    var policy = Policy.Handle<HttpRequestException>()
                    .RetryAsync(3, (exception, count) =>
                    {
                        logger.LogWarning("Attempt {Count} to fetch data failed: {Message}", count, exception.Message);
                    });
```

```csharp
    return await policy.ExecuteAsync(async () => await
    httpClient.GetStringAsync(url));
}
```

By implementing retry logic, you can enhance the reliability of your asynchronous methods.

14.3.3 Graceful Degradation

Design your application to degrade gracefully in the event of failures. This can involve providing fallback mechanisms or default values when a service call fails.

Example of Graceful Degradation:

```csharp
Copy code
public async Task<string> FetchDataWithFallbackAsync(string url)
{
    try
    {
        return await httpClient.GetStringAsync(url);
    }
    catch (HttpRequestException)
    {
        return "Default Data"; // Fallback value
    }
}
```

This approach ensures that the application remains functional, even when errors occur.

14.4 Documentation and Code Comments

Clear documentation is crucial for maintaining asynchronous code, especially as the codebase evolves. This section discusses the importance of documentation and effective commenting practices.

14.4.1 Documenting Asynchronous Methods

Document the purpose, parameters, return values, and exceptions for each asynchronous method. This information helps other developers understand how to use the method correctly and what to expect.

Example of XML Documentation:

```csharp
Copy code
/// <summary>
/// Fetches data from the specified URL asynchronously.
/// </summary>
/// <param name="url">The URL to fetch data from.</param>
/// <returns>A task that represents the asynchronous operation, containing the fetched data.</returns>
/// <exception cref="HttpRequestException">Thrown when an error occurs while fetching data.</exception>
public async Task<string> FetchDataAsync(string url);
```

Proper documentation enhances maintainability and reduces the learning curve for new developers.

14.4.2 Using Code Comments Wisely

While code comments can be beneficial, they should not be overused. Aim to write self-explanatory code and use comments to clarify complex logic or document important decisions.

Example of Effective Code Comments:

```csharp
Copy code
// Using Polly to implement retry logic for transient errors
var policy = Policy.Handle<HttpRequestException>().RetryAsync(3);
```

Avoid comments that simply restate what the code does; instead, focus on providing context and rationale.

14.5 Team Collaboration and Code Reviews

Collaboration within development teams is essential for maintaining high-quality asynchronous code. This section discusses strategies for effective teamwork and code reviews.

14.5.1 Establishing Coding Standards

Define and document coding standards for asynchronous programming

CHAPTER 14: BEST PRACTICES FOR MAINTAINING ASYNCHRONOUS CODE...

within your team. This should include naming conventions, error handling practices, and guidelines for structuring asynchronous methods.

14.5.2 Conducting Code Reviews

Implement a code review process that focuses on asynchronous programming patterns. Encourage reviewers to look for potential pitfalls, such as blocking calls or inadequate error handling.

Example Code Review Checklist:

- Are asynchronous methods suffixed with "Async"?
- Are all await statements correctly implemented?
- Is error handling implemented correctly?
- Are appropriate logging and documentation present?

14.5.3 Knowledge Sharing Sessions

Organize regular knowledge-sharing sessions where team members can discuss asynchronous programming best practices, share experiences, and present new tools or techniques. This fosters a culture of learning and continuous improvement.

Conclusion

In this chapter, we explored best practices for maintaining asynchronous code in C#12, covering various aspects crucial for long-term success. Key topics discussed include:

- Organizing asynchronous code for clarity and maintainability through meaningful naming conventions, grouping related methods, and refactoring long methods.
- Performance monitoring and optimization strategies, including implementing logging, profiling asynchronous code, and using Application Insights.
- Effective error handling practices, such as using try-catch blocks, implementing retry logic, and designing for graceful degradation.

- The importance of documentation and code comments for enhancing maintainability.
- Strategies for team collaboration, including establishing coding standards, conducting code reviews, and organizing knowledge-sharing sessions.

By adopting these best practices, developers can create high-quality, maintainable asynchronous applications that stand the test of time. Asynchronous programming continues to play a vital role in modern software development, and mastering these techniques will enable you to build responsive and efficient applications that meet the demands of today's users.

In the next chapter, we will explore emerging trends and future directions for asynchronous programming in C#, discussing the impact of new technologies and methodologies on the development landscape.

Chapter 15: Emerging Trends and Future Directions in Asynchronous Programming with C#12

Asynchronous programming has evolved dramatically over the past few years, driven by advancements in technology, changing developer needs, and the growing complexity of modern applications. This chapter explores emerging trends and future directions in asynchronous programming with C#12, examining the implications of these trends for developers and the industry as a whole.

15.1 The Rise of Asynchronous Streams

One of the most notable advancements in asynchronous programming is the introduction of asynchronous streams in C# 8.0. Asynchronous streams provide a way to handle data that arrives over time, allowing developers to process data incrementally and asynchronously.

15.1.1 Understanding Asynchronous Streams

Asynchronous streams combine the power of IAsyncEnumerable<T> with the await keyword, enabling developers to iterate over data in an asynchronous manner. This is particularly useful for scenarios involving real-time data processing, such as streaming data from APIs or handling large datasets.

Example of Asynchronous Streams:

```csharp
Copy code
public async IAsyncEnumerable<string> GenerateNumbersAsync()
{
    for (int i = 0; i < 100; i++)
    {
        await Task.Delay(100); // Simulate asynchronous work
        yield return i.ToString();
    }
}
```

In this example, the GenerateNumbersAsync method yields numbers asynchronously, allowing consumers to process them one at a time without blocking the main thread.

15.1.2 Applications of Asynchronous Streams

Asynchronous streams open up new possibilities for developers. Some potential applications include:

- **Real-Time Data Processing**: Stream data from IoT devices or sensors and process it in real time.
- **Incremental Data Loading**: Load large datasets incrementally, allowing users to interact with partial results while the rest of the data loads in the background.
- **Event-Driven Architectures**: React to events in real time by processing streams of data emitted by various components.

By leveraging asynchronous streams, developers can build responsive applications that handle data more efficiently.

15.2 Reactive Programming and Event-Driven Architectures

Reactive programming is gaining traction as a paradigm that simplifies the development of event-driven applications. The combination of asynchronous programming with reactive principles provides powerful tools for building responsive and resilient systems.

CHAPTER 15: EMERGING TRENDS AND FUTURE DIRECTIONS IN...

15.2.1 Introduction to Reactive Programming

Reactive programming focuses on the propagation of change, allowing developers to build applications that respond to data changes and user interactions seamlessly. This is achieved through the use of observables, which represent asynchronous data streams that can be observed and acted upon.

Example of a Reactive Observable:

```csharp
Copy code
var observable = Observable.Interval(TimeSpan.FromSeconds(1));
observable.Subscribe(x => Console.WriteLine($"Tick: {x}"));
```

In this example, an observable emits ticks every second, demonstrating how reactive programming allows developers to handle time-based events easily.

15.2.2 Benefits of Reactive Programming

The adoption of reactive programming brings several benefits:

- **Improved Responsiveness**: Applications can react to changes in data and events without blocking the main thread, resulting in a more fluid user experience.
- **Simplified Complexity**: Reactive programming helps manage complexity by allowing developers to express asynchronous flows declaratively.
- **Enhanced Composability**: Reactive extensions (Rx) provide a rich set of operators that enable developers to compose complex asynchronous workflows easily.

15.2.3 Event-Driven Architectures

Combining asynchronous programming with reactive principles leads to the development of event-driven architectures. In such architectures, components communicate through events, allowing for loose coupling and scalability.

Example of an Event-Driven Architecture:

- Use message queues (e.g., RabbitMQ, Azure Service Bus) to handle communication between services.
- Implement event sourcing to capture state changes as a sequence of events.

By adopting event-driven architectures, organizations can build scalable systems that respond dynamically to user actions and external events.

15.3 The Impact of Cloud-Native Development

Asynchronous programming is closely tied to cloud-native development, which emphasizes building applications designed to run in the cloud. This approach leverages cloud services, microservices, and containerization to enhance scalability and resilience.

15.3.1 Benefits of Cloud-Native Applications

Cloud-native applications are designed for flexibility and scalability. Key benefits include:

- **Elastic Scalability**: Asynchronous programming allows cloud-native applications to scale out easily by handling multiple concurrent requests without blocking resources.
- **Resilience and Fault Tolerance**: Asynchronous patterns enable applications to handle failures gracefully, retrying operations or using fallback strategies.
- **Continuous Deployment**: Cloud-native applications can be deployed continuously, allowing for rapid updates and iterations.

15.3.2 Leveraging Asynchronous Programming in Microservices

Microservices architectures benefit significantly from asynchronous programming. Each microservice can handle requests independently, allowing for high throughput and resilience.

Example of Asynchronous Communication Between Microservices:

- Use asynchronous messaging systems (e.g., Kafka, RabbitMQ) to facilitate communication between services.

CHAPTER 15: EMERGING TRENDS AND FUTURE DIRECTIONS IN...

- Implement service discovery to allow services to find and communicate with each other asynchronously.

By utilizing asynchronous programming within microservices, developers can build scalable, resilient applications that meet the demands of modern software development.

15.4 Advancements in .NET and C# for Asynchronous Programming

The .NET ecosystem continues to evolve, introducing new features and enhancements that make asynchronous programming more powerful and accessible. This section explores some of the key advancements in .NET and C# related to asynchronous programming.

15.4.1 Improved Performance and Efficiency

Recent updates to .NET have focused on improving the performance of asynchronous I/O operations and memory management. These enhancements contribute to the overall efficiency of asynchronous applications.

Key Improvements:

- **Memory Management**: Optimizations in the garbage collector and memory allocation reduce overhead for asynchronous applications, improving responsiveness.
- **I/O Performance**: Enhancements to asynchronous I/O operations lead to lower latency and higher throughput for network and file I/O.

15.4.2 New Language Features

C# continues to evolve, introducing new language features that enhance the asynchronous programming experience. Some potential features include:

- **Async Main Method**: C# 7.1 introduced the ability to use async in the Main method, allowing developers to write asynchronous console applications more easily.

Example of Async Main:

```csharp
Copy code
public static async Task Main(string[] args)
{
    await SomeAsyncMethod();
}
```

- **Pattern Matching Enhancements**: Improved pattern matching features can simplify the handling of exceptions and other asynchronous patterns.

15.4.3 New Libraries and Tools

The ecosystem surrounding asynchronous programming continues to grow, with new libraries and tools emerging to simplify development. Key areas of focus include:

- **Reactive Extensions (Rx)**: Libraries that provide a powerful framework for building asynchronous and event-driven applications.
- **Polly**: A .NET resilience and transient-fault-handling library that allows developers to implement retry policies and circuit breakers easily.

15.5 The Future of Asynchronous Programming in C#

As we look ahead, the future of asynchronous programming in C# holds exciting possibilities. This section discusses potential directions for asynchronous programming, considering advancements in technology, user expectations, and industry trends.

15.5.1 Increased Emphasis on Real-Time Applications

As user expectations evolve, there is a growing demand for real-time applications that provide instant feedback and updates. Asynchronous programming will play a crucial role in enabling developers to create applications that meet these demands.

Examples of Real-Time Applications:

- **Collaborative Tools**: Applications that allow multiple users to work together in real time (e.g., Google Docs) will rely heavily on asynchronous programming to ensure smooth interactions.
- **Gaming**: Multiplayer games require real-time communication between players and servers, making asynchronous programming essential for maintaining responsiveness.

15.5.2 The Integration of AI and Machine Learning

The integration of artificial intelligence (AI) and machine learning (ML) into applications presents unique challenges and opportunities for asynchronous programming. Asynchronous techniques will be crucial for handling long-running ML model training processes, allowing applications to remain responsive during computation-heavy tasks.

Example:

- Use asynchronous programming to perform predictions using pre-trained models while continuing to serve user requests.

15.5.3 Advancements in Quantum Computing

While still in its infancy, quantum computing promises to revolutionize many fields, including asynchronous programming. As quantum computing technology matures, developers may need to adopt new paradigms for handling concurrency and asynchronous operations.

Potential Impact:

- **Quantum Algorithms**: As quantum algorithms emerge, they may provide new ways to approach asynchronous problems, requiring developers to adapt their skills and techniques.

15.6 Conclusion

In this chapter, we explored emerging trends and future directions in asynchronous programming with C#12. Key topics discussed include:

- The rise of asynchronous streams and their applications in real-time data processing.
- The benefits of reactive programming and event-driven architectures for building responsive applications.
- The impact of cloud-native development on asynchronous programming practices and scalability.
- Advancements in .NET and C# that enhance the asynchronous programming experience, including performance improvements and new language features.
- The future of asynchronous programming in the context of real-time applications, AI integration, and potential developments in quantum computing.

By staying informed about these trends and embracing new technologies, developers can continue to build efficient, responsive, and scalable applications that meet the demands of modern software development. Asynchronous programming is a vital skill that will only become more critical as the landscape of technology continues to evolve.

In the final chapter, we will summarize the key takeaways from this book and reflect on the importance of asynchronous programming in today's development landscape.

Conclusion

Asynchronous programming has transformed the landscape of software development, enabling developers to build responsive, efficient, and scalable applications. This book has provided an in-depth exploration of asynchronous programming techniques in C#12, emphasizing their significance and practical applications in real-world scenarios. In this conclusion, we will recap the key concepts covered throughout the book, reflect on the importance of asynchronous programming, and offer final thoughts on how to continue evolving as a developer in this dynamic field.

Key Concepts Recap

Throughout this book, we have explored a wide range of topics related to asynchronous programming, providing developers with the tools and knowledge needed to harness the power of asynchronous patterns effectively. Here are the key concepts we've covered:

1. **Understanding Asynchronous Programming**: We established the fundamental principles of asynchronous programming, distinguishing it from synchronous programming. Asynchronous programming allows for non-blocking operations, improving application responsiveness and user experience.

2. **Task-Based Asynchronous Pattern (TAP)**: The introduction of TAP in C# 5.0 revolutionized asynchronous programming by allowing

developers to use the async and await keywords, making asynchronous code more readable and maintainable.
3. **Error Handling and Resilience**: We emphasized the importance of robust error handling in asynchronous applications, discussing best practices for managing exceptions and implementing retry logic to enhance application resilience.
4. **Performance Monitoring and Optimization**: Performance monitoring is critical for identifying bottlenecks in asynchronous code. We discussed strategies for logging, profiling, and using tools like Application Insights to ensure optimal performance.
5. **Testing Asynchronous Code**: Testing asynchronous methods requires different approaches than traditional synchronous testing. We explored best practices for unit testing, integration testing, and the use of mocking frameworks.
6. **Advanced Topics**: The book covered advanced topics such as asynchronous streams, reactive programming, and event-driven architectures, showcasing how these concepts can be integrated into modern application development.
7. **Real-World Applications**: We examined various real-world applications of asynchronous programming, including building scalable web APIs, responsive desktop applications, data processing pipelines, and real-time chat applications.
8. **Emerging Trends**: We discussed the future of asynchronous programming, highlighting trends such as the rise of asynchronous streams, the integration of reactive programming, the impact of cloud-native development, and advancements in the .NET ecosystem.

The Importance of Asynchronous Programming

Asynchronous programming is not just a programming model; it represents a fundamental shift in how developers build applications. The importance of asynchronous programming can be summarized as follows:

- **Enhanced User Experience**: In an age where users expect immediate

responses from applications, asynchronous programming allows developers to create responsive user interfaces that remain fluid and engaging, even during long-running operations.
- **Scalability and Efficiency**: Asynchronous programming enables applications to handle a high volume of concurrent requests without requiring a proportional increase in resources. This is particularly crucial for cloud-native applications and microservices architectures.
- **Real-Time Capabilities**: With the rise of real-time applications, asynchronous programming provides the necessary foundation for building systems that can react dynamically to events and changes in data, improving interactivity and engagement.
- **Adaptability to Modern Architectures**: Asynchronous programming aligns seamlessly with modern architectural patterns, such as event-driven and microservices architectures, making it an essential skill for developers in the contemporary software landscape.

Final Thoughts

As you embark on your journey with asynchronous programming in C#12, consider the following recommendations:

1. **Continue Practicing**: Asynchronous programming is a skill that improves with practice. Build projects that utilize asynchronous patterns, experiment with different techniques, and explore the capabilities of C#12 to deepen your understanding.
2. **Stay Informed**: The technology landscape is constantly evolving. Keep abreast of new features, libraries, and best practices related to asynchronous programming. Follow industry blogs, participate in online communities, and engage with fellow developers to share insights and experiences.
3. **Focus on Code Quality**: Write clean, maintainable asynchronous code. Prioritize readability, documentation, and error handling to ensure that your codebase is robust and easy to understand.
4. **Embrace New Patterns and Technologies**: Asynchronous program-

ming is a dynamic field, with new paradigms and technologies emerging regularly. Be open to adopting new approaches, such as reactive programming and asynchronous streams, to enhance your development capabilities.

5. **Collaborate and Share Knowledge**: Work with your peers to share knowledge and experiences related to asynchronous programming. Engage in code reviews, participate in knowledge-sharing sessions, and contribute to a culture of learning within your team.

In conclusion, asynchronous programming is an indispensable skill for modern developers, empowering them to create applications that are responsive, scalable, and capable of meeting the demands of today's users. By mastering the techniques and concepts outlined in this book, you will be well-equipped to harness the full potential of asynchronous programming in C#12 and continue to thrive in the ever-evolving world of software development.

www.ingramcontent.com/pod-product-compliance
Lightning Source LLC
Chambersburg PA
CBHW071025240526
45469CB00006BD/2089